Great Cake Places
LONDON2012

Edited by
Jeffrey Young & Jacqueline Malouf

Author: Allegra Strategies
Photography: Maximillian Gower
& Madelaine Warwick
Design: John Osborne
Website: Tim Spring
Other content: Sarah Edwards
Publisher: Allegra Publications Ltd

Allegra
PUBLICATIONS

Published by *Allegra* PUBLICATIONS Ltd © 2011
No.1 Northumberland Ave, Trafalgar Square, London, WC2N 5BW

Visit our website:
www.greatcakeplaces.com

All information was accurate at time of going to press.

Foreword

As a budding young chef training in Sydney followed by Paris, I visited London for the first time in the 1980s. I had no idea I would spend so many years of my life in this great city, but I am glad I have. Back in 1986, London was not a genuinely inspiring place for food culture and was even less so for desserts, cakes and pastries. Celebrity chefs were not yet heard of, unless they came from France.

Fish and chips, and pie and mash were among the best British cuisine had to offer. With the exception of a few enlightened venues, simple and uninspiring sponge cakes and stodgy puddings were served unashamedly and the British public took little interest in delicious, crafted food. For a young, ambitious cook who desired to work and learn from the best it was time to look abroad.

A decade later in 1996, I returned to London to discover a fledgling food culture. Delia was in her prime, and Jamie, Nigella and others were now featured on TV and starting to become household names. This was the beginnings of something profoundly revolutionary for British food and baking.

Today an explosion of artisan bakeries, third-wave cafés, fine patisseries and a newly flourishing afternoon tea segment, not to mention the colourful American-style cupcakeries, place London as one of the leading cities for the enjoyment of cakes.

With some of the world's grandest hotels, and some of the edgiest and most inspiring street markets, London has something to offer every taste. Life is there to be lived to its fullest, and in the words of Dr. Samuel Johnson: 'there is in London all that life can afford.'

Based on all the innovation and acceleration of interest in baking and cooking I have seen only in the past few years, I feel the best is still ahead, and that it will move very fast from here. Already a place full of great cake places, London is destined for further sweet success.

Enjoy!

Jeffrey Sheridan Young

Contents

Great Cake Place Ratings

Every venue that appears in Great Cake Places has been visited and rated by our expert team. The ratings fall into two separate categories: Cake Rating and Overall Rating.

Ratings are given for Cupcakes and Bakery, Coffee and Cake, and Afternoon Tea venues only.

RATINGS

CAKE
4.75 / 5

OVERALL
3.25 / 5

Cake Rating

The Cake Rating is not only about the taste, it takes into account numerous other 'cake credentials' such as the cake's presentation, visual appeal, innovation, level of skill involved and whether the cake is made in-house.

The following question is the guiding principle used to determine the Cake Rating:

To what extent does this cake place deliver an amazing 'cake' experience?

Overall Rating

In combination with the Cake Rating the Overall Rating considers to what extent the venue delivers a 'wow factor'. Elements that are taken into account include the atmosphere, design, customer service and display, among other factors.

To determine the Overall Rating the following question is used as the guiding principle:

How does the combination of the cake and cake store experience achieve exceptional levels of excitement for cake-lovers?

Key to icons

 Gluten free

 Organic products

 Dairy free

 Soya available

 Credit / debit cards accepted

 Toilets

 Mother and baby friendly

 Wheelchair access

 WiFi

 Licensed

 Reservations recommended

 Outdoor area

 Wedding cakes

 Pet friendly

The History Of Cakes

Cakes have a long and delicious history. The word "cake" is derived from the Norse word "kaka" which means "to cook". This term was first used to describe small, flat breads cooked on both sides, more like pancakes.

Cake later became fairly indistinct from breads, biscuits and buns, but the term was also used to refer to small or expensive breads for special occasions. During the 18th and 19th centuries, cakes again became more distinct as yeast was replaced with baking powder and beaten eggs as raising agents for cakes that resembled light sponges.

Most ancient cultures made some form of cake, although these would have more closely resembled a biscuit, a fried or sweet bread, or a cheesecake. For instance, small baked items similar to oat cakes have been found by archaeologists in Neolithic villages.

According to food historians, the ancient Egyptians were the world's first accomplished bakers, serving breads sweetened with honey at feasts to invoke Hathor, the goddess of love, beauty, motherhood and joy. These treats often contained a plentiful mixture of dried fruits and nuts.

The Greeks ate "plakous" (meaning "flat breads") which were combinations of nuts and honey. It is thought from the writings of Cato that the Romans developed two types of cakes often used as offerings to the gods. A "libum" was a honey and cheese bread, similar to a biscuit, that was scented with bay leaves, while "placenta" was a pie-like pastry made with honey and ricotta, also lined with bay leaves.

The Romans are believed to have developed the first fruit cakes which were then brought to Britain. In his writings, 14th century writer Geoffrey Chaucer describes immense special occasion cakes containing butter, cream, eggs, spices, currants and honey.

Cupcakes & Bakery

The History Of Cupcakes

The first mention of the term 'cupcake' appeared in Eliza Leslie's 'Seventy-Five Receipts for Pastry, Cakes and Sweetmeats' in 1828. The term originally referred to both the container used to cook the small cake and the cupfuls of ingredients - such as butter, flour and sugar - used in the recipe. This uncomplicated method meant anyone could prepare the cakes, particularly since the earliest versions called for simple measurements equivalent to one cup of butter, two of sugar, three of flour and four of eggs. As a result, cupcakes were sometimes called "number cakes" or "1-2-3-4 cakes". Today, however, cupcake is a common term for any small, decorated cakes baked in paper cups.

Cupcakes have always been popular treats for children and are typically embellished with fun decorations, lots of sprinkles and sweet, brightly coloured icing. Often cupcakes are associated with the traditional era of homemaking in the 1950s and 1960s, but in truth, they are just as popular today than at any time in the past. The Magnolia Bakery in New York could be credited with making cupcakes the gourmet and fashionable item they are today, after Sex and the City characters Carrie and Miranda were seen biting into their cupcakes while having a girly gossip. Even after the end of that iconic series in 2004, cupcake fever continues to sweep London, with cake shops, cookbooks and cake-decorating classes continuing to prove popular with the city's fashionistas.

Did you know: Winston Churchill is said to be the first to suggest that plain cupcakes be topped with sweet icing instead of lard.

Bake-a-Boo

86 Mill Lane, NW6 1NL

*P*retty in pink, this petite bakery provides countless special treats for everyone, including a selection of delights free from wheat, gluten and dairy. The extensive menu introduces cake-lovers to an array of cute individually named delicacies, including Charlie the chocolate cake and Lola the lemon cupcake. Perfect for a hen party, afternoon tea or special treat with friends, the interior is packed with nostalgic floral tables and doilies, pastel-coloured shelves and vintage chandeliers. Founder Zoe Berkeley personalises the Bake-a-Boo experience with special touches including her cookbook, and crafts made by friends for sale in-store.

Afternoon Tea

Selection of finger sandwiches, scones with jam and cream, Boo's vanilla cupcakes, chocolate-dipped strawberries, mini brownies, teapot-shaped vanilla biscuits. All served on tiered cake stands with a pot of tea.

£15.00 per person

Signature Cake

Victoria Sponge Cake
£2.20

Open

Mon-Tues.	Closed
Weds-Thur.	2:00pm - 6:00pm
Fri.	12:00pm - 6:00pm
Sat.	10:00am - 6:00pm
Sun.	12:00pm - 6:00pm

Overview

Year Opened
2006
Owner
Zoe Berkeley
Pastry Chef
Zoe Berkeley & team

Suppliers

Tea Supplier
W Martyn and Brewhaha
Coffee Supplier
Illy

Price Range

Cupcakes   £1.85 - £2.25

Contact

020 7435 1666
www.bake-a-boo.com
info@bake-a-boo.com

CAKE
3.75 / 5

OVERALL
3.75 / 5

Buttercup Cake Shop

16 Saint Alban's Grove, W8 5BP

Cupcakes & Bakery

*T*his brightly decorated hotspot contains every type of beautifully decorated cupcake imaginable. The interior blazes with bright shades of lime, yellow and pink. The gorgeous goodies are hand-crafted using the finest ingredients and flavours include chocolate purist and bounty, as well as other lavish options such as fantasy - a rich vanilla cake topped with streaked vanilla buttercream icing and sprinkles. A personalised cake service allowing customers to order bespoke cakes is also available. The service is as delightful as the cupcakes.

Contact

020 7937 1473
www.buttercupcakeshop.co.uk
yum@buttercupcakeshop.co.uk

Sister Locations

Westfield Stratford City and White City, Bluewater

Open

Mon-Fri.	8:45am - 5:00pm
Sat.	10:00am - 5:00pm
Sun.	Closed

Overview

Year Opened
2007
Owner
Donna Egan

Suppliers

Tea Supplier
The London Tea Company
Coffee Supplier
The Natural Coffee Co

Signature Cake

Fantasy Cupcake
£2.50

Price Range

Cupcakes   £2.50 - £3.00

CAKE
3.75 / 5

OVERALL
3.50 / 5

RATING

Cake Boutique

31 Lavender Hill, SW11 5QW

Decorated in hues of incandescent white, Cake Boutique is one of Lavender Hill's most popular venues. Customers are greeted with a delicious aroma and a display of delights laid out on a grand marble platform. Artistically decorated cupcakes are finished with skill and care, and the brilliant shades of lemon, raspberry and blueberry icing entice. Adorable embellishments top off the culinary creations - meticulously placed sprinkles and raspberry hearts add the perfect touch. Fruit cake fanatics can delight in the Cake Boutique's rendition of this classic, made from an old family recipe. The rustic interior features white-washed wooden floorboards complemented with light table tops and splashes of red. Exuding an atmosphere of calm, this family-friendly hangout is extremely popular with local mums.

Contact

020 7228 0023
www.cakeb.com
info@cakeb.com

Open

Mon-Fri.	7:30am - 7:00pm
Sun.	8:30am - 7:00pm

Overview

Year Opened
2011
Owner
Banu Ezer

Signature Cake

Walnut & Banana Cupcake
£1.90

Suppliers

Tea Supplier
Tea Palace
Coffee Supplier
Lavazza

Price Range

Cupcakes	£1.70

RATING

CAKE
3.50 / 5

OVERALL
3.50 / 5

Cat & the Cream

Unit 10, Heliport Estate, Bridges Court, Battersea, SW11 3RE

Images supplied by Cat & the Cream

Cat & the Cream creates luxury handcrafted cakes using organic, natural and Fairtrade ingredients. Named after founder Cat Lyne, Cat & the Cream caters for any occasion. The unique menu is comprised of an array of chocolate and fruity cupcake delights. Chocolate favourites include the dark chocolate and cherry vegan chocolate cakes, while fruity options extend to the delicious strawberry, chai and pistachio. Layers of luxurious, creamy icing, often accompanied by impeccably placed embellishments add the finishing touch. Cakes can be made to order and are also found in high-end food outlets including Whole Foods. Cat & the Cream's perfectly packaged delights are beautifully presented in a translucent box specifically designed to keep cakes in pristine condition.

Contact

075 2828 5717
www.catandthecream.com

Open

By appointment only

Overview

Year Opened
2007
Owner
Cat Lyne
Pastry Chef
Cat Lyne

Price Range

Cupcakes   £2.50 - £2.95

RATING

CAKE
3.75 / 5

OVERALL
3.25 / 5

Cox Cookies & Cake

13 Brewer Street, W1F 0RH

The worlds of fashion and baking collide at Cox Cookies & Cake, which is led by former shoe designer Patrick Cox. The avant-garde treats showcased within are novel, creative and more often than not naughty. Dazzlingly decorated cupcakes are available, but the triple-X-rated range of Coxxx Cakes set this store apart. The popular beef cake features a butch hazelnut praline cake and icing topped with a bulging bicep. Perfect for hen parties or birthdays, Cox Cookies & Cake provides cake lovers with a fun alternative. The shop design features screaming neon and leather themes that are apt given its location in Soho's red-light district.

Suppliers

Tea Supplier
Twinings
Coffee Supplier
Miko

Contact

020 7434 0242
www.coxcookiesandcake.com
info@coxcookiesandcake.com

Open

Sun-Thur.	11:00am - 8:00pm
Fri-Sat.	11:00am - 11:00pm
Sun.	12:00pm - 6:00pm

Overview

Year Opened
2010
Owner
Patrick Cox

Signature Cake
Titty Cake
£4.00

Price Range

Cupcakes   £2.50 - £4.00

RATING

CAKE
3.50 / 5

OVERALL
3.75 / 5

Ella's Bakehouse
20a The Piazza, WC2E 8RB

Ella's Bakehouse is the brainchild of former international supermodel Lorraine Pascale. Swapping the catwalk for cupcake couture, Pascale's flourishing business is comprised of beautifully decorated cakes and brownies. A bright pink and red interior is teamed with 1960s milk bar decor. An incandescent rouge chandelier is warm and inviting, and kisses on the wall are a sweet touch. The cherry on top is row after row of magical sparkling cupcakes including the mini cherry crumble, which is deliciously moist and generously iced. Cake addicts should also note the rich and creamy Oreo Cake. Customers can perch on cute red stools and people-watch across the lively Covent Garden piazza and those who fancy a drink can take their pick from the fresh juice or coffee options. Cakes are beautifully packaged and are available in store or online.

Signature
Cake

Oreo Cake
£2.75

Open

Mon-Sat.	10:00am - 7:00pm
Sun.	10:00am - 6:00pm

Overview

Year Opened
2009
Owner
Lorraine Pascale
Pastry Chef
Lorraine Pascale & team

Suppliers

Tea Supplier
Twinings
Coffee Supplier
Musetti

Price Range

Coffee & Cake	£4.30+
Cupcakes	£2.50 - £2.75

Contact

075 4082 4082
www.ellasbakehouse.co.uk
info@ellasbakehouse.co.uk

CAKE
4.00 / 5

OVERALL
3.75 / 5

Hummingbird Bakery Spitalfields

11 Frying Pan Alley, E1 7HS

TOP
20

*T*he Hummingbird Bakery is famous for providing London cake lovers with impeccable American-influenced cupcakes, moist layer cakes and whoopie pies. The menu offers an array of cupcake flavours including vanilla, chocolate and carrot, all topped with flawless, luxurious icing. Among the most popular is the bakery's signature red velvet cupcake, a deliciously moist confection with cream cheese frosting. The latest addition to The Hummingbird Bakery family is this Spitalfields store, which features a modern and spacious interior in Hummingbird's trademark chocolate and pink colour scheme. Specialised cake consultants and bakers are available for those in need of one-off designs. Cupcake lovers will enjoy a memorable experience at this exciting new location.

Sister Locations

Notting Hill, Soho and South Kensington

Open

| Mon-Fri. | 8:30am - 6:30pm |
| Sat-Sun. | 11:00am - 6:00pm |

Overview

Year Opened
2004
Owner
Tarek Malouf

Suppliers

Tea Supplier
Teapigs
Coffee Supplier
Illy

Price Range

| Cupcakes | £2.00 - £2.95 |

Contact

020 7851 1795
www.hummingbirdbakery.com
telesales@hummingbirdbakery.com

Signature Cake
Red Velvet
Cupcake
£2.65

RATING

CAKE
4.25 / 5

OVERALL
4.25 / 5

Lily Vanilli

The Bakery, 6 The Courtyard, Ezra Street, E2 7RG

*L*ocated off the beaten track near Columbia Road Flower Market, this shabby-chic bakery is the brainchild of graphic designer turned cake creator Lily Jones, whose client list includes Elton John and Nigella Lawson. Known for her ability to create unconventional designs, Lily is also the go-to girl for high-impact special occasion cakes – Halloween, for example, is one of her many specialties. The bakery stocks traditional cupcakes and cakes in an array of delicious flavours such as the delectable red velvet with coconut, redcurrant cake and the triple chocolate brownie. The space itself is cosy and provides cake lovers with the chance to mingle with creatives and enjoy edible creations. Lily is also a promoter of Fairtrade ingredients and holds cooking classes by appointment at her store each Saturday.

Find Lily Vanilli's Bakewell Tarts and Vanilla Buttercream recipe on page 148

Signature Cake
Bakewell Tart
£3.00

Open

Sun.	8:30am - 4:30pm

Overview

Year Opened
2009
Owner
Lily Jones
Pastry Chef
Lily Jones & team

Suppliers

Tea Supplier
Clipper and We Are Tea
Coffee Supplier
Coleman Coffee

Price Range

Cupcakes   £2.00 - £3.00

Contact

www.lilyvanilli.com
sendflours@lilyvanilli.com

RATING

CAKE
4.25 / 5

OVERALL ★ ★ ★ ★
4.00 / 5

Lola's Cupcakes

16 Lansdowne Row, W1J 8QF

*T*his cute cake shop specialises in lavish, handcrafted cakes for all occasions. Artfully decorated, cupcakes are topped with creamy icing and embellished with pretty pastel sprinkles and innovative edible images. Flavours include traditional favourites, as well as the more indulgent rocky road and choc coconut. Those after special occasion cupcakes can look to Lola's Pink Label range, for which sophisticated flavours are topped with elegant touches. Chocolate lovers can treat themselves to the mint chocolate truffle cupcake, a rich chocolate confection with peppermint icing and a gourmet white mint chocolate on top. Coffee enthusiasts can delight in the deliciously moist coffee cappuccino pearl cupcake, topped with coffee buttercream icing, cappuccino pearls and an Americano truffle. The interior is simple yet stylish, with a blue and white colour scheme creating a light and breezy ambiance. Limited seating is also available.

Sister Locations

Selfridges, Topshop
and Harrods

Signature
Cake

Red Velvet
Cupcake
£2.50

Open

Mon-Fri.	8:00am - 7:00pm
Sat.	8:00am - 6:00pm
Sun.	Closed

Overview

Year Opened
2007
Owner
Victoria Jossel & Romy Lewis

Suppliers

Tea Supplier
Clipper Teas
Coffee Supplier
Union Hand-Roasted

Price Range

Cupcakes   £2.50 - £4.00

Contact

020 7483 3394
www.lolas-kitchen.co.uk
hello@lolas-kitchen.co.uk

RATING

CAKE
4.00 / 5

OVERALL
3.50 / 5

18

Love Bakery

319 King's Road, SW3 5EP

*L*ove Bakery is the tale of Samantha Blears and the sensation her cakes caused at her childrens' school fair. This success led to a catering business, which then blossomed into the cupcake boutique Blears dazzles her customers with today. Exuding down-to-earth chic and with a myriad of colourful delights on display, Love Bakery's interior is bright, sparkling and filled with candy-coloured treats topped with elaborate fondant decorations. Love's cupcake menu has something for everyone - inspired by seasonal flavours, cake fiends can opt for the ever-changing flavour of the day or one of the popular staples including vanilla, chocolate, and lemon and rose. Eschewing commercial equipment in favour of domestic mixers and traditional methods, Blears and her helpers have maintained a homemade approach.

Signature Cake

Red Velvet
Cupcake
£2.00

19

Open

Mon-Sat.	10:30am - 6:00pm
Sun.	Closed

Overview

Year Opened
2009
Owner
Samantha Blears & John Love

Suppliers

Tea Supplier
Various
Coffee Supplier
Various - Fairtrade

Price Range

Coffee & Cake	£2.65 - £4.50
Cupcakes	£1.65 - £3.00

Contact

020 7352 3191
www.lovebakerylondon.com

Find Love Bakery's Lemon Cupcakes recipe on page 153

RATING

CAKE
4.00 / 5

OVERALL
3.75 / 5

Molly Bakes

Netil Market, 11-25 Westgate Street, E8 3RL

Cupcakes & Bakery

*M*olly Bakes sells an array of cupcakes based on her mother's secret recipe at Netil Market, just around the corner from Broadway Market. Creative treats including cake pops, layer cakes, brownies, mini tarts, bespoke cakes and pies are also available. Subscribing to her theory that "cakes should taste as good as they look and look as good as they taste", Molly's creations are delicious works of art. Cakes contain premium ingredients including British butter, Fairtrade cocoa, free-range eggs and unrefined sugar. Among the spectacular cake pop creations are the pretty tea party pops and more quirky moustache pop and sushi pop. Luxurious cupcake bouquets and dessert tables are also available. Molly's celebrity client list includes Lady Gaga and Elle Macpherson.

Contact

www.mollybakes.co.uk
info@mollybakes.co.uk

Open

Sat.	11:00am - 6:00pm

ORGANIC

Signature Cake

Cake Pops and Truffles
£2.00 each

Overview

Year Opened
2009

Price Range

Cupcakes	£2.00 - £3.50

RATING

CAKE
3.75 / 5

OVERALL
3.25 / 5

Ms Cupcake

408 Coldhabour Lane, SW9 8LF

*M*s Cupcake's dream is to bake decadent cupcakes and layer cakes for the masses, which she does, in over 100 flavours. With a sliding scale of the weird and wonderful, lovers of more conventional classics can enjoy old favourites such as raspberry ripple or banoffee. For those wanting to take a walk on the wild side, more outlandish flavours such as mojito and Earl Grey Tea are available. Ms Cupcake's cakes are also all vegan and her Brixton store was one of the first vegan cake shops in London, but her cakes all have moist textures and lose nothing in terms of flavour. An extensive gluten-free range is also available. Service comes with a sparkling smile and treats can be enjoyed on the run or in an outside seating area.

Contact

www.mscupcake.co.uk
info@mscupcake.co.uk

Open

Mon-Tues.	11:00am - 6:00pm
Weds-Sat.	11:00am - 7:00pm
Sun.	11:00am - 5:00pm

Overview

Year Opened
2011
Owner
Ms Cupcake

Price Range

Cupcakes £2.20

Signature Cake

Ferrero Rocher Cupcake
£2.20

RATING

CAKE
3.75 / 5

OVERALL
3.75 / 5

The Old Post Office Bakery

76 Landor Road, SW9 9PH

At the forefront of the organic bread movement, The Old Post Office Bakery is the brainchild of founder John Dungavel. Breads, cakes and hot treats are baked with love on site each day. Containing organic ingredients, the range includes baked treats such as carrot cake, gluten-free orange cake, fresh pastries and croissants. Homemade slices, brownies and a range of organic breads are also available. As its name suggests, the bakery is located within an old wooden post office and the interior is cosy, just big enough to stock the array of British favourites within.

Sister Locations

Greensmiths Waterloo

Signature Cake

Apple & Almond Cake
£1.60

Open

| Mon-Sat. | 7:00am - 6:00pm |
| Sun. | 7:00am - 2:00pm |

Overview

Year Opened
1982
Owner
John Dungavel & Richard Scroggs
Pastry Chef
Idirs Agboola

Price Range

Cupcakes   £1.75 - £3.55

Contact

020 7326 4408
www.oldpostofficebakery.co.uk
enquires@oldpostofficebakery.co.uk

RATING

CAKE
3.25 / 5

OVERALL
3.25 / 5

SMALL ORGANIC
RYE
SOURDOUGH
£1.10

ORGANIC
RYE & SUNFLOWER
SOURDOUGH
£1.85

ORGANIC
MALTED GRAIN
LOAF
£1.65

ORGANIC
WHOLEWHEAT
LOAF
£1.45

24

Primrose Bakery

69 Gloucester Avenue, NW1 8LD

An institution among cake addicts, Primrose Bakery serves homely American-inspired treats to both local kids and the young-at-heart. The signature cupcake range includes both traditional and experimental options: malt and marshmallow, peanut butter, and rose and ginger are among the more creative. The delightfully decorated cupcakes are topped with buttercream icing and sparkling sprinkles. The store's ambiance is as joyous as the primrose yellow shopfront promises, and cakes are as delicious as the amazing aroma within. Cakes are accompanied by nostalgic beverage options such as a Coke float, a glass of organic cold milk or a selection of teas. Fun purchases such as pretty wrapping paper and Justin Bieber memorabilia are also sold.

Sister Locations

Covent Garden

Signature Cake

Strawberry Cake
£2.60

Open

Mon-Sat.	8:30am - 6:00pm
Sun.	10:00am - 5:30pm

Overview

Year Opened
2004
Owner
Martha Swift & Lisa Thomas

Suppliers

Tea Supplier
Dammann Press Tea and Mariage Freres
Coffee Supplier
Allpress

Price Range

Coffee & Cake	£4.50 - £5.00
Cupcakes	£1.85 - £2.50

Contact

020 7483 4222
www.primrosebakery.org.uk
primrose-bakery@btconnect.com

RATING

CAKE
4.00 / 5

OVERALL
4.00 / 5

Treacle

110-112 Columbia Road, E2 7RG

*S*et within one of the East End's oldest markets on Columbia Road, Treacle is a nostalgic temptation that is impossible to resist. Treacle describes itself as an unashamed celebration of basic British baking and the menu is a no-nonsense selection of cupcakes and comfort food. The interior is basic, reflecting Treacle's homage to a simpler bygone era and its best sellers are the large cupcakes in lemon, vanilla and chocolate flavours. Cakes are beautifully iced in pink, cream, baby blue or mint green and topped with sprinkles. A limited selection of beverages is also available - tea is a year-round staple, while homemade lemonade and organic elderflower cordial are available during summer. Displays of wonderful vintage and contemporary design knick-knacks top off the retro experience.

Contact

020 7729 0538
www.treacleworld.com
enquiries@treacleworld.com

Open

| Sat. | 12:00pm - 5:00pm |
| Sun. | 9:30am - 3:30pm |

Overview

Year Opened
2003
Owner
Bux Bailey

Suppliers

Tea Supplier
Rosy Lee

Price Range

| Cupcakes | £1.00 - £2.50 |

RATING

CAKE
3.75 / 5

OVERALL
3.50 / 5 ★★★⯪

Coffee
& Cake

Albion

2-4 Boundary Street, E2 7DD

Attached to Shoreditch's Boundary Hotel, Albion is a buzzing culinary precinct comprised of a bakery, a restaurant and a small shop selling British goods. Tantalising aromas waft from the kitchen, as cupcake aficionados decide what treats to taste. Ravishing displays of biscuits and cakes prevail, although the straightforward savoury options are tempting too. Deli shelves burst with artisanal takeaway delights. Set in a converted warehouse, the dining area is spacious and airy, extending to the outside pavement where more seating is provided. Muted tones complement the exposed brick and white walls, while long communal wooden tables encourage neighbourly mixing and mingling. Opposite Shoreditch House, Albion is the perfect place to people-watch or catch up with friends.

Open

Daily:	8:00am - 11:30pm

Overview

Year Opened
2008
Owner
Sir Terence Conran & Peter Prescott
Pastry Chef
Jenny Cekaj

Suppliers

Tea Supplier
Howard
Coffee Supplier
L'Unico

Price Range

Coffee & Cake	£5.45 - £7.45
Cupcakes	£2.50

Contact

020 7729 1051
www.albioncaff.co.uk
info@prescottandconran.com

RATING

CAKE
3.75 / 5

OVERALL
4.00 / 5

Baker & Spice Chelsea

47 Denyer Street, SW3 2LX

*A*cclaimed for its outstanding cakes and pastries, Baker & Spice makes its sweets on site from scratch using only the finest ingredients. Decadent displays of freshly baked sponge cakes, fruit flans, meringues and brownies tempt customers. Crowd pleasers include the delicious blueberry baked cheesecake, croissants, pecan slice and luxuriously iced chocolate cupcakes. The rustic interior features wooden hues, mouth-watering sweet treats and savoury fare. With a family-friendly and relaxed atmosphere, this is a wonderful place for coffee and cake lovers to meet friends and relax.

Sister Locations

Belgravia, Maida Vale and Selfridges

Signature Cake

Carrot Cake
£5.25

Open

Mon-Sat.	7:00am - 7:00pm
Sun.	8:00am - 6:00pm

Overview

Year Opened
1995
Owner
Patisserie Holdings Ltd
Pastry Chef
Vladmir Ovcarik

Suppliers

Tea Supplier
Suki
Coffee Supplier
Miko

Price Range

Coffee & Cake   £4.00 - £9.00

Contact

020 7225 3417
www.bakerandspice.uk.com

CAKE
4.00 / 5

OVERALL
4.00 / 5

Bea's of Bloomsbury
Theobald's Road

*H*igh-quality, unique and made with love, Bea's of Bloomsbury cakes are impossible to resist. Greeted with a counter display of enticing American-influenced cakes and treats, customers can immediately see that this establishment genuinely cares about its food. Cakes are made with only the best-quality ingredients and cake lovers can accompany treats with Jing tea and Valrhona chocolate. A sophisticated yet quirky afternoon tea selection includes a cake stand full of mini baguettes, scones and delicious treats, but Bea's is famous for its cupcakes and the most popular flavours include delicious lamington, ultimate chocolate fudge and passion fruit vanilla. Scrumptious cheesecakes and a daily selection of additional cakes are also available.

Afternoon Tea

Mini savoury baguettes, scones with jam and cream, signature cupcakes, marshmallow, mini Valrhona brownie, mini Belgian blondie, mini meringue and pot of Jing tea.

£15.00 per person

Find Bea's of Bloomsbury's Meringues recipe on page 154

TOP 20

44 Theobold's Road, WC1X 8NW

Open

Mon-Fri.	8:00am - 7:00pm
Sat-Sun.	12:00pm - 7:00pm

Overview

Year Opened
2008
Owner
Bea Vo
Pastry Chef
Kate Donnan

Suppliers

Tea Supplier
Jing Tea
Coffee Supplier
Square Mile Coffee Roasters

Price Range

Coffee & Cake	£5.00 - £6.00
Cupcakes	£1.50 - £4.00

Contact

020 7242 8330
www.beasofbloomsbury.com
contact@beasofbloomsbury.com

RATING

CAKE
4.50 / 5

OVERALL
4.25 / 5

Belle Epoque Patisserie

37 Newington Green, N16 9PR

Belle Epoque is a traditional French patisserie situated on Newington Green. Located in a breathtaking building that dates back to 1856, the café features authentic decor and shelves spilling over with French produce and exquisite cakes. Patrons have the choice of dining in a tea room or secluded garden. The setting is splendid, but the food and cakes remain the real draw. Owners Eric Rousseau and his wife Hülya handpick all the ingredients used in each pastry and viennoiserie. Every item is made by experienced pastry chefs using traditional French techniques to ensure creations are of the highest quality.

The signature Belle Epoque cake with an orange crème brulée centre is a taste of heaven and the towering Croquembouche is as spectacular as the macarons are delicate.

Open

Mon.	Closed
Tues-Fri.	8:00am - 6:00pm
Sat.	9:00am - 6:00pm
Sun.	9:00am - 5:00pm

Overview

Year Opened
2002
Owner
Eric Rousseau & Hülya Rousseau
Pastry Chef
Frank Turban

Suppliers

Tea Supplier
Twinings
Coffee Supplier
Molinari and Tudor

Price Range

Coffee & Cake   £4.80 - £5.75

Contact

020 7249 2222
www.belleepoque.co.uk
info@belleepoque.co.uk

Signature Cake

Belle Epoque
Cake
£3.95

RATING

CAKE
4.50 / 5

OVERALL
4.25 / 5

Betty Blythe

73 Blythe Road, W14 0HP

Betty Blythe delivers a quintessentially English tea-time experience with a hint of glamour. Named after one of Hollywood's earliest screen sirens, this intimate tea room features enchanting decor, a fine food pantry spilling over with delights and a treasure trove of vintage clothes and relics. The menu is seasonally inspired, offering a selection of colourful cupcakes, decadent biscuits and sweet treats. A selection of sandwiches and gourmet deli treats are available for those who prefer savoury fare. Waitresses are delightful and dressed to impress. Perfect for a charming tea party or an afternoon indulgence with friends, the Betty Blythe experience is worth the trip.

Afternoon Tea

Selection of finger sandwiches, mini scones, selection of cakes and biscuits including chocolate brownies and mini cupcakes, and tea or coffee.

£20.00

Contact

020 7602 1177
www.bettyblythe.co.uk
darling@bettyblythe.co.uk

Open

| Mon-Sat. | 8:00am - 6:00pm |
| Sun. | Private bookings only |

Overview

Year Opened
2008
Owner
Lulu Gwynne

Suppliers

Tea Supplier
Sherston Tea
Coffee Supplier
Rizzi Coffee

Signature Cake
Carrot cake
£2.80

Price Range

| Coffee & Cake | £4.90+ |
| Cupcakes | £2.40 - £2.80 |

RATING

CAKE
3.25 / 5

OVERALL
3.50 / 5

Black Vanilla

32 Tranquil Vale, SE3 0AX

This boutique bakery and gelateria sells delicious treats handmade with care. Sourcing the finest ingredients to produce premium delights, Black Vanilla uses imported chocolate, Lescure butter and Madagascan bourbon vanilla. Desserts on offer include baked cakes and fresh gelato, and the delicious gelato whoopie pie comprised of two soft chocolate cakes filled with delicious Italian ice cream. Cake enthusiasts can sit within the contemporary interior featuring dark wooden furniture and stainless steel light hangings. Although the venue buzzes with energy, the atmosphere is genuinely relaxed. Sweet treats can be accompanied by Black Vanilla's freshly ground coffees.

Contact

020 8852 0020
www.black-vanilla.com
info@black-vanilla.com

Sister Locations

Greenwich Village

Open

| Mon-Fri. | 8:00am - 5:30pm |
| Sat-Sun. | 8:00am - 6:00pm |

Overview

Year Opened
2011
Owner
Milton Lee
Pastry Chef
Jo Stone

Suppliers

Tea Supplier
Choi Times
Coffee Supplier
Allpress

Signature Cake

Black Vanilla
Chocolate Cake
£2.25

Price Range

Coffee & Cake £4.00-£6.00

RATING

CAKE
3.50 / 5

OVERALL
3.75 / 5

Brownie Box

247 Old Brompton Road, SW5 9HP

*R*un by sisters Niki and Kristi Markou, Brownie Box is an old-fashioned cake boutique specialising in scrumptious brownies and blondies. Carefully baked with love, the creations are made using long-standing family recipes. Among the best-sellers is the brownie muffin, a melt-in-the-mouth chocolate muffin with real chocolate chunks and the famous original brownie, a soft yet chewy chocolate brownie filled with milk chocolate pieces. Cakes, cupcakes, muffins and cookies are also on offer. Located in Earl's Court, the cosy shop has a warm and friendly atmosphere.

Afternoon Tea

Three-tier cake stand consisting of mini cupcakes, brownie bites and mini cakes.

£6.00 - £8.00

Price Range

Coffee & Cake	£2.80 - £3.10
Cupcakes	£2.20 - £2.60

Contact

020 7373 9111
www.browniebox.co.uk
brownieboxon247@gmail.com

Open

Mon-Fri.	8:30am - 8:00pm
Sat.	9:00am - 9:00pm
Sun.	10:00am - 8:00pm

Overview

Year Opened
2011
Owner
Kristi Markou

Suppliers

Tea Supplier
Dammann Press Tea
Coffee Supplier
Illy

Signature Cake

Original Brownie
£1.80

RATING

CAKE
3.75 / 5

OVERALL
3.75 / 5

Caffé Concerto Haymarket

45 Haymarket, SW1Y 4SE

$\mathcal{T}$his luxurious Italian dining experience offers exquisite handmade cakes, pastries and gâteaux. In a contemporary dining room in the heart of London, Caffé Concerto Haymarket welcomes dessert lovers with a front window display of decadent inspired creations and sweet treats. Perfect for a business meeting or a catch-up with friends, among Caffé Concerto's most popular treats are the delicious selva gâteau, a chocolate sponge with crème pâtisserie and mixed fruits, and the rich and creamy vanilla and chocolate mousse. Located amid many of London's theatres and museums, this venue features opulent mirrors and café-style seating, as well as lavish leather booths.

Afternoon Tea

Cream Tea
Scones, mini tartlets and a hot beverage.

£8.50

Afternoon Tea
Sandwiches, scones, assorted tarts and selected teas.

£14.50

Contact

0844 335 8403
www.caffeconcerto.co.uk
haymarket@caffeconcerto.co.uk

Sister Locations

10 locations around London

Open

Daily:	7:30am - 11:00pm

Overview

Year Opened
2009
Owner
Mohamad Borjak

Suppliers

Tea Supplier
Mighty Leaf
Coffee Supplier
Mokarabia

Price Range

Coffee & Cake   £7.75+

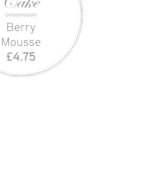

Signature Cake

Berry Mousse
£4.75

RATING

CAKE
4.00 / 5

OVERALL
3.75 / 5

Cake Boy

Unit 2 Kingfisher House, Battersea Reach, Juniper Drive, SW18 1TX

*S*triving to make the world a sweeter place, Cake Boy is a luxurious cake emporium showcasing divine desserts. Cakes are freshly baked and dreamily decorated daily by award-winning master patissier Eric Lanlard. Often changing to meet customer demand for new and exciting treats, the menu includes irresistible delights such as the best-selling chocolate sacher and lemon tart. Another favourite is the rich and velvety chocolate mousse, a mousse dome with a crunchy praline base, embellished with lashings of ornately decorated chocolate. Situated in a tranquil, contemporary new development alongside the Thames, Cake Boy's glamorous interior features rich colours, subtle damask-influenced patterns, bold chandeliers and brightly coloured armchairs. Baking enthusiasts can also attend the Cake Boy Cookery School, run by the master patissier himself, but be sure to book well in advance.

Afternoon Tea

Selection of mini pastries, French macarons, mini deli sandwiches, selection of organic tea or coffee and a glass of champagne.

£30

Open

Mon-Fri.	8:00am - 6:00pm
Sat.	9:00am - 6:00pm
Sun.	Closed

Overview

Year Opened
2007
Owner & Pastry Chef
Eric Lanlard

Suppliers

Tea Supplier
Town & Country Fine Foods
Coffee Supplier
Puro Fairtrade Organic

Price Range

Coffee & Cake	£4.05 - £7.00
Cupcakes	£1.50 - £1.80

Contact

020 7978 5555
www.cake-boy.com
miki@cake-boy.com

Signature Cake

Valrhona Dark Chocolate
& Raspberry Torte
£3.55

*Find Cake Boy's
Orange and Lavender Cake
recipe on page 155*

RATING

CAKE
4.75 / 5

OVERALL
4.50 / 5

Coffee & Cake

Ca'puccino

138a King's Road, SW3 4XB

*O*ffering an assortment of imported Italian delights, Ca'puccino is one of the newest additions to London's cake scene. Exuding a modern and relaxed ambiance, the Chelsea store offers a range of irresistible Sal De Riso Costa D'Amalfi house pastries and desserts. Chocolate lovers can indulge in the tortina di farro cioccolato e noci, a deliciously rich treat made using high-quality melted chocolate and walnuts. Ice cream aficionados can delight in the creamy ice cream made on site each morning using fresh seasonal ingredients. The most popular flavours include yoghurt, coffee and pistachio. A range of pastries and croissants are also available, as is an extensive coffee menu. Spacious in feel, customers can sit back and relax in generous white leather chairs, while colourful stacked book columns are featured upstairs and down. The oversized tea cups and saucers perched on the front counter add a memorable finishing touch.

Contact

020 7036 0555
www.ca-puccino.com
info@ca-puccino.com

Sister Locations

Westfield London and Harrods

Open

Daily:	8:00am - 10:00pm

Overview

Year Opened
2011
Owner
Giacomo Moncalvo
Pastry Chef
Salvatore De Riso

Suppliers

Tea Supplier
Twinings
Coffee Supplier
House blend from Brazil

Price Range

Coffee & Cake   £5.85 - £7.10

Signature Cake

Tiramisù
£4.05

CAKE
3.75 / 5

OVERALL
3.75 / 5

RATING

The Chelsea Teapot

402 King's Road, SW10 0JL

A charming haven with a doll's house feel, The Chelsea Teapot offers scrumptious cupcakes, delectable sweet treats and thoroughly English fare. Cake lovers are spoilt for choice, with an impressive array of beautifully presented delights on show in the front window. The elegant tower of luxuriously iced cupcakes features flavours including red velvet, chocolate, lemon and banana. Moist in texture and delicious in taste, cakes are made from locally sourced and organic ingredients (where possible). Perfect for a relaxing catch-up with friends or a special occasion, The Chelsea Teapot is tucked away from London's hustle and bustle. The quaint interior features pretty pastels and delicate finishing touches, including novelty teapots, vintage antiques and carefully selected cake gifts. A lovely way to celebrate baby showers, hen nights or birthdays, The Chelsea Teapot also hosts a range of special events including afternoon teas, cupcake decorating and tarot readings.

Afternoon Tea

Selection of finger sandwiches, homemade scones served with Rodda's clotted cream & strawberry jam, cakes, pastries and a pot of tea.

£17.50

Contact

020 7751 5975
www.thechelseateapot.com
info@thechelseateapot.com

Open

Mon.	Closed
Tues-Fri.	8:30am - 6:30pm
Sat.	9:30am - 6:30pm
Sun.	12:00pm - 6:30pm

Overview

Year Opened
2009
Owner
Melissa Montezani

Suppliers

Tea Supplier
Dammann Press Tea
Coffee Supplier
Illy

Signature Cake

Mini Victoria Sponge
£5.00

Price Range

Coffee & Cake	£5.00+
Cupcakes	£2.50

RATING

CAKE
4.00 / 5

OVERALL
4.00 / 5

Chez Le Boulanger

178 Upper Street, N1 1RG

This independent French pâtisserie is one of Islington's new gems. Hidden behind the bright red signage out front is a cosy coffee and cake haven with a raw, rustic feel. A display of French pastries and delectable delights are displayed in the front glass window and on the counter. The setting possesses a quaint country house ambiance complete with exposed brick, polished wooden floors and sturdy timber furnishings. Accessorised with an array of kitchen condiments, canisters and chalked blackboards, cake lovers can devour treats in a homely atmosphere. Free wifi is also available.

Contact

020 7354 3399

Open

Daily:	7:00am - 10:00pm

Overview

Year Opened
2011

Suppliers

Tea Supplier
Various - Fairtrade
Coffee Supplier
Bozanero

Price Range

Coffee & Cake   £5.50 - £6.50

RATING

CAKE
3.50 / 5

OVERALL
3.50 / 5

Dolly's

Lower ground floor, Selfridges & Co, 400 Oxford Street, W1A 1AB

evisiting the romantic encounters of Selfridges founder Harry Selfridge, this charming cafe is named after his lovers, the identical twin sisters Rosika and Jansci Deutsch who were known as the Dolly Sisters. Located at the heart of Selfridges' lower ground floor, the café offers cakes, pastries and a selection of teas and coffees. Comprised of a selection of traditional British cakes, the menu ranges from chocolate cake and brownies to classic Victoria sponge and cupcakes. Savoury options such as open sandwiches and light salads are also available. Decadent in feel, the interior boasts a Roaring Twenties theme, in homage to its infamous namesakes.

Afternoon Tea

Cream Tea

Scones with Selfridges jam and clotted cream and a pot of tea.

£8.50

Afternoon Tea

Finger sandwiches, scones with Selfridges jam and clotted cream, Belle Epoque pastries and a pot of Selfridges tea.

£20.95

Champagne Afternoon Tea

The Afternoon Tea with a glass of Esprit Brut Champagne.

£29.95

Contact

020 7318 3616

Open	
Mon-Wed.	9:30am - 8:30pm
Thur-Fri.	9:30am - 9:00pm
Sat.	9:30am - 8:30pm
Sun.	11:30am - 6:00pm

Overview

Year Opened
2011
Owner
Selfridges

Suppliers

Tea Supplier
L'Unico
Coffee Supplier
Mussetti

Price Range

Coffee & Cake   £5.90 - £9.45

RATING

CAKE
4.25 / 5

OVERALL
4.25 / 5

SELECTION OF
CLASSIC CUPCAKES

3.95
EACH

Drink, Shop & Do

9 Caledonian Road, N1 9DX

Located just around the corner from the chaos of King's Cross, Drink Shop & Do is a haven of crafts, cakes, coffee, candy and vintage nostalgia housed inside an old Victorian-era Turkish bathhouse. What first appears to be a small store selling gifts, craft supplies and sweets actually opens into a light and spacious cafe and vintage furniture emporium decorated with fairy lights, bright Formica, quirky china and retro patterns. A range of homemade cakes and candies are displayed on the vintage-style bar and the extremely friendly and helpful staff prepare a range of dainty sandwiches, fine teas, Torino Espresso coffee and frankly delicious cocktails for their mostly female clientele. Craft events, hen parties and afternoon teas are available by appointment.

Contact

020 3343 9138
www.drinkshopdo.com

Open

Mon-Fri.	10:30am - 11:00pm
Sat.	10:30am - 12:00am
Sun.	10:30am - 8:00pm

Overview

Year Opened
2010
Owner
Kristie Bishop & Coralie Sleap

Suppliers

Tea Supplier
All About Tea
Coffee Supplier
Torino Espresso

Price Range

Coffee & Cake	£5.00+
Cupcakes	£3.00

RATING

CAKE
3.50 / 5

OVERALL
3.75 / 5 ★★★⯪☆

Fleet River Bakery

71 Lincoln's Inn Fields, WC2A 3JF

$\mathscr{T}$his homely bakery creates an irresistible range of homemade treats on-site, from scratch. Cake lovers are treated to an ever-changing selection of muffins, biscuits, cheesecakes, slices, tarts and pastries. Splendidly presented on shiny silver and green cake stands, offerings include nostalgic favourites such as jam flapjacks, or the moist carrot cake topped off with delicious cream cheese icing. The rustic homespun interior is set across two levels and features large arched windows and a timber motif throughout. Perfect for a casual catch-up with friends or family, sweet tooths can sit in the cosy area inside or at the tables outside. Treats are accompanied by a delicious blend of Monmouth coffee served by trained baristas.

Price Range

Coffee & Cake	£4.70
Cupcakes	£3.30

Contact

020 7691 1457
www.fleetriverbakery.com
info@fleetriverbakery.com

Open

Mon-Fri.	7:00am - 7:00pm
Sat.	9:00am - 5:00pm
Sun.	Closed

Overview

Year Opened
2009
Owner
Jon Dalton

Suppliers

Tea Supplier
Emeyu
Coffee Supplier
Monmouth

RATING

CAKE
4.25 / 5

OVERALL
4.00 / 5

Gail's Exmouth Market

33-35 Exmouth Market, EC1R 4QL

*G*ail's is a bakery and delicatessen that specialises in artisan breads, pastries and luscious cakes. The light-filled spacious interior features exposed brickwork and has a modern feel. The central display of cakes spills over with freshly baked sweet gems and gourmet delights. Artisan breads are clearly a major focus, but a decadent range of baked goods are also on offer including chocolate tarts, fondants and seasonally inspired cakes. The mouth-watering pastries are free of preservatives, colours and additives. Among favourites are the carrot cake and chocolate cake. Gail's Exmouth Market also offers Jing Tea, Union coffee, wine and beer.

Contact

020 7713 6550
www.gailsbread.co.uk
exmouthmarket@gailsbread.co.uk

Sister Locations

Battersea, Chiswick, Crouch End, Hampstead, Notting Hill, Queen's Park, South Kensington and St John's Wood

Open

Mon-Fri.	7:00am - 7:00pm
Sat-Sun.	8:00am - 7:00pm

Overview

Year Opened
2010
Owner
Ran Avidan & Tom Molnar
Pastry Chef
Oded Tomin

Suppliers

Tea Supplier
Jing Tea
Coffee Supplier
Union Hand-Roasted

Price Range

Coffee & Cake   £5.50+

Signature Cake
Baked Cheesecake
£3.50

RATING

CAKE
4.50 / 5

OVERALL
4.25 / 5

Garden Museum

The Garden Café, 5 Lambeth Palace Road, SE1 7LB

A tranquil retreat from the outside world, the Garden Museum café is set in a 17th century-style knot garden among lush maple and tulip trees. This peaceful haven is the perfect place for cake lovers to catch up and unwind with a garden-inspired menu that often uses fresh herbs and seasonal ingredients from the garden itself. Chocolate lovers can treat themselves to creations including the gooey dark chocolate, hazelnut and cherry brownie, or the chocolate beer cake. Fruit lovers may choose to explore delicious options including the plum frangipane, or the gluten-free whole orange and rosemary cake. Delights are freshly baked on-site each day. Espresso coffee is available to accompany treats. Booking is required for groups of 10 or more and café guests can dine without paying admission for exhibitions.

Open

Sun-Fri.	10:30am - 5:00pm
Sat.	10:30am - 4:00pm

Overview

Year Opened
1978
Owner
Christopher Woodward
Pastry Chef
Sorrel Ferguson

Suppliers

Tea Supplier
Drury
Coffee Supplier
Drury

Price Range

Coffee & Cake   £5.50 - £7.00

Contact

020 7401 8865

Signature Cake
Orange & Lavender Cake
£2.95

RATING

CAKE
3.75 / 5

OVERALL
4.00 / 5

ORANGE
LEMON
LAVENDER

Ginger & White

4a-5b Perrins Court, NW3 1QS

This self-described "British coffee shop" is a calm oasis nestled in a charming Hampstead side street. Inspired by farmers markets and artisan producers across Britain, the cake menu is comprised of classics including lemon drizzle loaf, Eccles cakes and the classic Victoria sponge. Families or ladies who lunch can settle at the rustic communal table within a modern and uncomplicated yet heritage British interior. Worn floors and slouchy leather couches work in with modern light fixtures and monochrome hues. A muted-tone painting of the British flag hangs high on the wall. Cakes can be accompanied by sublime Square Mile coffees, and savoury fare and condiments - including homemade peanut butter - are also available.

Contact

020 7431 9098
www.gingerandwhite.com
info@gingerandwhite.com

Open

Mon-Fri.	7:30am - 5:30pm
Sat-Sun.	8:30am - 5:30pm

Overview

Year Opened
2009
Owner
Tonia George, Nicholas Scott & Emma Scott

Suppliers

Tea Supplier
Jing Tea
Coffee Supplier
Square Mile Coffee Roasters

Price Range

Coffee & Cake	£5.30 - £7.30
Cupcakes	£1.80 - £3.00

CAKE
4.00 / 5

OVERALL
4.00 / 5

RATING

The Haberdashery

22 Middle Lane, N8 8PL

Find The Haberdashery's
Rhubarb and Amaretto Cake
recipe on page 156

Coffee & Cake

This quirky eatery, coffee house and vinyl outlet is set within a renovated Victorian shop that was restored to its 1920s glory by The Haberdashery's founders and friends. The menu is filled with delectable homemade cakes baked using local ingredients. Muffins are beautifully presented in terracotta pots, soft drinks are served in mason jars and sweet lovers can treat themselves to the Art Deco haberdashery counter stuffed with retro confectionery. The interior is delightfully eclectic, with a toy-meets-teashop feel. Mismatched vintage dishes and mosaics of Victorian fireplace tiles are also special touches. A hub of creativity, The Haberdashery is a favourite with local artists and craftspeople and organises a wide range of popular community events. The regular Haberdashery car boot sales see the venue converted into a vintage bric-a-brac market complete with cocktails and live music.

Contact

020 8342 8098
www.the-haberdashery.com
info@the-haberdashery.com

Open

Mon-Fri.	8:00am - 6:00pm
Sat-Sun.	9:00am - 6:00pm

Overview

Year Opened
2009
Owner
Greg Vukasovic & Massimo Bergamin
Pastry Chef
Alberto Carballo

Suppliers

Tea Supplier
W Martyn
Coffee Supplier
Bristot

Signature Cake

Rose & Elderflower Cake
£3.95

Price Range

Coffee & Cake   £4.25 - £8.00

RATING

CAKE
3.75 / 5

OVERALL
3.75 / 5   ★★★⯪☆

Kaffeine

66 Great Titchfield Street, W1W 7QJ

This independent café offers seasonal baked treats and a menu that changes weekly, meaning loyal customers are presented with a sweeping selection of pastries, cakes, friands, tarts and biscuits. Chocolate fanatics can often choose from the white chocolate blondie or super-moist chocolate brownies. Fruit lovers, however, are not forgotten, nor are those who prefer savoury muffins. Kaffeine's expert baristas are committed to using their Synesso machine to provide loyal customers with the perfect cup of Square Mile coffee and despite its location near to bustling Oxford Street, a laidback antipodean atmosphere dominates. Coffee and cake lovers can populate wooden benches and stools, listen to music and watch the world pass by. Service is cheerful, with Kaffeine achieving its objective - to maintain a standard based on genuine hospitality. Breakfast, brunch and lunch are available.

Contact

020 7580 6755
www.kaffeine.co.uk
kaffeine@live.co.uk

*Find Kaffeine's
Banana Bread recipe
on page 149*

Open

Mon-Fri.	8:00am - 6:00pm
Sat.	9:00am - 6:00pm
Sun.	10:00am - 5:00pm

Overview

Year Opened
2009
Owner
Peter Dore-Smith

Suppliers

Tea Supplier
Teapigs
Coffee Supplier
Square Mile Coffee Roasters

Price Range

Coffee & Cake   £3.10 - £4.50

CAKE
4.00 / 5

OVERALL
4.25 / 5

RATING

Konditor & Cook Stamford Street

63 Stamford Street, SE1 9NB

With best-sellers including Curly Whirly chocolate vanilla cake and trademark double chocolate chip brownies, it's no wonder Konditor & Cook has acquired a cult following. Founder and culinary innovator Gerhard Jenne has designed a collection Nigella Lawson describes as: "Fabulous cakes, the sort you'd make yourself if only you had the time, energy or inclination." The Stamford Street shop is filled with decadent homemade treats including frosted sponge cakes, fruit tarts, tempting slices and magic cakes. Ornately packaged biscuits and a range of bespoke celebration cakes are also available. Committed to quality, organic ingredients are used where possible. The deep mulberry storefront and olde worlde decor within adds warmth. The hot chocolate combines Valrhona Couverture with double cream and is the perfect accompaniment to any treat.

Contact

0844 854 9371
www.konditorandcook.com
stamfordstreet@konditorandcook.com

Sister Locations

Borough Market, Chancery Lane, Soho, The Swiss Re Building and Waterloo

Open

Mon-Fri.	7:30am - 6:00pm
Sat.	10.00am - 5.30pm
Sun.	Closed

Overview

Year Opened
2009
Owner
Gerhard Jenne

Suppliers

Tea Supplier
Teapigs and Yorkshire Tea
Coffee Supplier
Drury

Signature Cake

Curly Whirly Cake
£2.75

Price Range

Coffee & Cake   £4.65 - £6.15

RATING

CAKE
4.00 / 5

OVERALL
4.00 / 5   ★★★★☆

L'Eto Caffe
155 Wardour Street, W1F 8WG

TOP 20

Meaning "summer" in Russian, L'Eto provides cake lovers with a truly inspiring array of beautifully prepared cakes and desserts. On London's bustling Wardour Street, the café's front window overflows with a selection including tarts, cakes and slices. The vibrantly coloured blackcurrant delice cassis is a delectable sweet caramel biscuit base layered with a light, tart, blackcurrant mousse and topped with a jelly glaze. A recent addition to London's cake scene, L'Eto Caffe is already buzzing. The perfect catch-up destination for a meeting with friends or a colleague, the café also serves savoury snacks and a range of beverages. Wait staff are attentive, prices are reasonable, service is over the counter and the experience comes with perks - loyalty cards and wifi.

Open

Mon-Tues.	9:00am - 9:00pm
Wed-Sat.	8:00am - 11:00pm
Sun.	9:00am - 9:00pm

Overview
Year Opened
2011
Owner
Alexander Login

Suppliers
Tea Supplier
Metropolitan Tea
Coffee Supplier
Allpress

Price Range
Coffee & Cake   £5.50+

Contact
020 7494 4991
letocaffe@gmail.com

Signature Cake
Honey Cake
£3.80

CAKE
4.50 / 5

OVERALL
4.00 / 5

RATING

Ladurée Harrods

87/135 Brompton Road, SW1X 7XL

Image supplied by Ladurée

The story of the Ladurée macaron started early in the 20th century when founder Louis Ernest Ladurée's second cousin took two macaron shells and joined them with a ganache filling. Today, macarons remain Ladurée's most famous creation. Located within the chic surroundings of Harrods, this iconic tearoom serves macarons, millefeuilles and tarts galore. Heavenly macaron flavours include the popular caramel with salted butter, rose and blackcurrant violet.
The opulent marble decor and rainbow-coloured array of pastel sweets create an opulent atmosphere and wait staff are attentive and accommodating of dietary requirements.

Afternoon Tea

Selection of finger sandwiches, mini viennoiseries, pastries and a choice of coffee, tea or hot chocolate.

£21.00

Contact

020 3155 0111
www.laduree.fr
salesuk@laduree.com

Sister Locations

Cornhill, Covent Garden and Burlington Arcade

Open

Mon-Sat.	9:00am - 9:00pm
Sun.	11:30am - 6:00pm

Overview

Year Opened
2005
Owner
David Holder

Suppliers

Tea Supplier
Ladurée
Coffee Supplier
Ladurée

Price Range

Coffee & Cake   £6.50 - £9.50

RATING

CAKE
4.25 / 5

OVERALL
4.50 / 5

Lanka

71 Regents Park Road, NW1 8UY

TOP 20

Lanka offers premium, fastidiously presented cakes, made in-house by chef Masayuki Hara. This cake shop and tea salon in leafy Primrose Hill features minimal decor and an impressive glass display of Japanese-inspired desserts. Created using imagination and skill, the cake collection includes the delectable Green Tea Tart: subtle in flavour and delicate in texture, the tart is filled with a light, velvety green tea filling, topped with delicate white chocolate shavings. Another delicious option is the Chocolate Bread and Butter Pudding. A large selection of more traditional French gâteaux, tarts, mousses and macarons are offered. Drinks including Monmouth coffee and loose-leaf teas imported from Sri Lanka complete the experience.

Suppliers

Tea Supplier
Euphorium Tea Salon
Coffee Supplier
Monmouth

Contact

020 7483 2544
www.lanka-uk.com
lanka.catering@btinternet.com

Open

Mon.	Closed
Tues-Sat.	8:00am - 8:00pm
Sun.	9:00am - 5:00pm

Overview

Year Opened
2010
Owner
Masayuki Hara & Mina Hara
Pastry Chef
Masayuki Hara

Signature Cake

Green Tea Chocolate Gateau
£3.60

Price Range

Coffee & Cake   £3.90 - £6.90

Find Lanka's Chocolate Bread & Butter Pudding recipe on page 150

RATING

CAKE
4.50 / 5

OVERALL
4.25 / 5 ★★★★✩

Loafing

79 Lauriston Road, E9 7HJ

This beautifully rustic neighbourhood café offers carefully sourced artisan sweet treats and breads. The front window is lined with colourful homemade delights perched on pretty cake stands - the collection includes indulgent cakes, tarts, brownies and muffins. Worthy of special mention are the popular lemon meringue cake and classic Victoria sponge. Cakes are accompanied by a range of Newby teas beautifully served in dainty vintage china teapots and cups, or Monmouth coffee. The provincial-themed interior has a personal feel and features clean white surfaces paired with wooden furniture, antique mirrors and a sparkling chandelier. Customers can sit in or outside in the intimate garden area. Vintage homewares and a selection of jams and gourmet condiments are also sold.

Signature Cake

Victoria Sponge
Cake
£3.50

Open

Mon-Fri.	7:30am - 6:00pm
Sat.	8:00am - 6:00pm
Sun.	9:00am - 6:00pm

Overview

Year Opened
2008
Owner
Susie McDuell

Suppliers

Tea Supplier
Newby
Coffee Supplier
Monmouth

Price Range

Coffee & Cake	£5.90 - £7.90
Cupcakes	£2.50 - £2.75

Contact

020 8986 0777
www.loafing.co.uk
info@loafing.co.uk

RATING

CAKE
4.25 / 5

OVERALL
4.00 / 5

66

Luca's Bakery

145 Lordship Lane, SE22 8HX

Exuding down-to-earth charm, Luca's Bakery specialises in freshly baked fare. The counter features a multitude of breads and an array of treats such as generously sized cinnamon buns, brownies and cheesecakes, just to name a few. Goodies can be washed down with beverages including coffee and homemade lemonade. Brunch, lunch and dinner is also offered. The interior is rustic, with dark, stripped-back wooden floorboards complemented by clean white walls. This is the perfect place to enjoy a quiet moment or visit with a group, and the communal tables create a strong sense of community. On a nice day, the tranquil and open setting out back is also a lovely option. Those in a hurry can opt to take away.

Contact

020 8613 6161
www.lucasbakery.com
bread@lucasbakery.com

Open

Mon-Sat.	8:30am - 5:30pm
Sun.	9:00am - 5:00pm

Overview

Year Opened
2008

Suppliers

Tea Supplier
Cup of Tea Ltd
Coffee Supplier
Volcano Coffee Works

Price Range

Coffee & Cake   £6.00

Signature Cake

Cinnamon Bun
£1.90

RATING

CAKE
3.75 / 5

OVERALL
3.75 / 5

Macaron Patisserie

22 The Pavement, SW4 0HY

Sit under the sky blue ceiling and enjoy the delicious treats this authentic French patisserie has on offer. Elegantly hand-crafted pastries, homemade ice cream and vibrantly coloured tarts shine from behind the glass display counter. Cake enthusiasts can peer into the kitchen through the small window behind the counter and see where the magic happens. Located on a peaceful edge of Clapham Common, the patisserie's decor features wood-panelled walls, a dark parquet floor and an antique chandelier. Large windows allow plenty of natural light and visitors can sit at their own small table or opt for the wooden communal dining option. Delights can be enjoyed with coffee or pots of tea.

Contact

020 7498 2636

Open

Mon-Fri.	7:30am - 7:00pm
Sat.	8:00am - 7:00pm
Sun.	9:00am - 7:00pm

Overview

Year Opened
2005
Owner
Bertrand Le Net
Pastry Chef
Medhi Gourini

Suppliers

Tea Supplier
Jing Tea
Coffee Supplier
Finest Pure Coffee

Price Range

Coffee & Cake   £3.00 - £4.00

RATING

CAKE
3.75 / 5

OVERALL
3.75 / 5 ★★★⯪☆

Maison Bertaux

28 Greek Street, W1D 5DQ

This London institution is not just a café – it is an experience. Full of character, the original decor exudes a unique and quirky retro charm and the warm relaxed atmosphere is largely thanks to its two owners, sisters Michele and Tania Wade. An original haven of individuality within trendy Soho, Maison Bertaux's tiny interior features mismatched chairs and eclectic art. Loyal guests are greeted with a beautiful front window display of generously portioned classic French pâtisserie and viennoiserie. Popular favourites include the delectable pain au chocolat and picture-perfect strawberry tarts. The high-quality creations are freshly baked on-site every day and takeaway treats are also available.

Afternoon Tea

Basic cream tea with scones and a pot of tea.
£6.20

Contact

020 7437 6007
www.maisonbertaux.com

Open

Mon-Fri.	8:30am - 11:00pm
Sat-Sun.	9:30am - 8:00pm

Overview

Year Opened
1871
Owner
Michele Wade & Tania Wade
Pastry Chef
George Nabil

Signature Cake

Mont Blanc
Cheesecake
£4.50

Suppliers

Tea Supplier
Langdon and various others
Coffee Supplier
Angelucci

Price Range

Coffee & Cake   £5.10 - £7.20

RATING		
CAKE 3.75 / 5		
OVERALL 3.75 / 5		

Maison Blanc Hampstead

76 High Street, NW3 1QX

Open

Mon-Thur.	7:30am - 7:30pm
Fri.	7:30am - 8:00pm
Sat.	8:00am - 8:00pm
Sun.	9:00am - 7:30pm

Overview

Year Opened
1981
Owner
Raymond Blanc

Suppliers

Coffee Supplier
Fairtrade

Price Range

Coffee & Cake   £4.50+

Afternoon Tea

Maison Blanc Afternoon Tea

Ten fine mini pastries and a coffee or a pot of tea.

£9.90

English Afternoon Tea

Homemade plain or fruit scones with a choice of toppings and a coffee or a pot of tea.

£4.90

𝓑ringing a small slice of France to London, Maison Blanc is an authentic French patisserie that serves freshly baked artisan breads, cakes and true French pastries. Founded by Michelin-starred chef Raymond Blanc, Maison Blanc's extensive cake range includes an array of French-inspired delights such as the indulgent chocolate éclair, which is made from choux pastry, chocolate crème pâtisserie and topped with chocolate fondant icing. Those after something fruitier can delight in best-seller Tart au Citron, a crisp butter pastry with a zesty lemon filling. Hampstead customers can sit on European-style seating out front, or enjoy treats inside amid the wooden-themed decor. A range of packaged sweets, condiments and coffee beans are also sold.

Contact

020 7443 9722
www.maisonblanc.co.uk
enquiries@maisonblanc.com

Sister Locations

14 other locations

RATING

CAKE
4.00 / 5

OVERALL
3.75 / 5

Mouse & de Lotz

103 Shacklewell Lane, E8 2EB

*N*amed after dynamic duo Nadia Mousawi and Victoria Shard (née de Lotz), this Dalston haunt sells a host of scrumptious homemade cakes, fresh sandwiches and Square Mile coffee. Pricing is reasonable, and baked goods are divine. Among the most popular are the toothsome tea loaf (with butter), chocolate tiffin and cappuccino walnut cake. Cakes on offer change from time to time and can include carrot cake, coconut cake with white chocolate and raspberry, and lemon or raspberry whoopies. The display is topped off with old-fashioned tags stamped with the café's signature mouse motif. Goodies are served on dainty, often mismatched china. The recently renovated interior oozes warmth - quaint and quirky touches such as chalked blackboards and cheekily defaced Victorian postcards complete the experience.

Open

Mon-Fri.	8:00am - 6:00pm
Tues.	Closed
Sat.	9:00am - 6:00pm
Sun.	10:00am - 6:00pm

Overview

Year Opened
2010
Owner
Nadya Mousawi & Victoria Shard

Suppliers

Tea Supplier
Yorkshire Tea
Coffee Supplier
Square Mile Coffee Roasters

Price Range

Coffee & Cake   £4.20 - £4.70

Contact

020 3489 8082
www.mousedelotz.com
info@mousedelotz.com

*Signature
Cake*

Chocolate
Tiffin
£2.00

CAKE
3.75 / 5

OVERALL
3.75 / 5

Coffee @ Cake

Napket Piccadilly

61 Piccadilly, W1J 0DY

The Napket experience offers fabulously high-quality food set within a fashionably urban interior. This versatile eatery caters for all daily needs: those on the run can opt for a quick takeaway coffee and treat in the morning, while ladies who lunch or those doing business can sit for a substantial meal or sweet treat. The buzzing ambiance, although reflective of fast-paced Piccadilly, remains relaxed. Mellow background jazz serenades customers as they sit back and enjoy the establishment's top-notch service. Open brick walls, dim lighting and grand chandeliers add warmth. The bakery offers ravishing treats including artisanal breads, delicious pastries and an afternoon tea collection. An allergy-friendly range is also available, including gluten, dairy and sugar-free brownies, cakes and muffins. A variety of coffees, international teas and juices are also available.

Contact

020 7493 4704
www.napket.com
napket-piccadilly@napket.com

Sister Locations

Vigo Street, Brook Street and Royal Exchange

Open

Daily:	8:00am - 7:00pm

Overview

Year Opened
2006
Owner
Eric Hanson

Suppliers

Tea Supplier
Jing Tea
Coffee Supplier
Lavazza

Signature Cake

Strawberry Tart
£4.50

Price Range

Coffee & Cake   £6.50 - £8.50

RATING

CAKE
3.75 / 5

OVERALL
4.25 / 5

Nordic Bakery Golden Square

14a Golden Square, W1F 9JG

ℒaunched in 2007 by Finnish-born Jali Wahlsten, Nordic Bakery is an understated but stylish establishment. Traditional Nordic sweets and a chic interior offer customers a taste of the wholesome, comforting style of Scandinavia. If the Boston cake doesn't appeal, the signature cinnamon bun will - this delight is comprised of layer upon layer of warm, buttery, spiced pastry. Treats can be enjoyed with a smooth, creamy Vibar coffee. The clientele is an eclectic mix of creative types. The design features dark blue walls teamed with wooden surfaces, polished cement floors, high ceilings and exposed ventilation to creates a modern, open, comfortable feel. Denim apron-clad wait staff take a similarly minimal approach to service, proving friendly but not overbearing.

Contact

020 3230 1077
www.nordicbakery.com
info@nordicbakery.com

Sister Locations

Marylebone

Open

Mon-Fri.	8:00am - 8:00pm
Sat.	9:00am - 7:00pm
Sun.	11:00am - 6:00pm

Overview

Year Opened
2007
Owner
Jali Wahlsten

Suppliers

Tea Supplier
Clipper Teas
Coffee Supplier
Vibar

Price Range

Coffee & Cake   £4.40 - £5.00

RATING

CAKE
3.50 / 5

OVERALL
3.75 / 5

The Orangery

Kensington Palace, Kensington Gardens, W8 4PX

Set in Kensington Palace's lush grounds, The Orangery provides a regal backdrop for an opulent sensory soiree. Guests can admire immaculately kept surroundings while enjoying the sweet treats on offer. The well-lit establishment, which was once Queen Anne's quarters, today features a master table overflowing with an assemblage of signature scones, traditional cakes, meringues and tarts. Those after a spot of tea are spoilt for choice: the British-grown collection includes a signature Afternoon at the Palace blend of single-estate Darjeeling and Chinese black teas. Those desiring an afternoon tea affair can choose from numerous alcoholic and non-alcoholic options.

Suppliers

Tea Supplier
Tregothnan and Newby
Coffee Supplier
Rainforest Alliance Coffee

Price Range

Coffee & Cake   £6.50 - £7.50
Cupcakes   £4.50

Contact

020 3166 6112
www.theorangery.uk.com
orangery@digbytrout.co.uk

Open

March to October:
Daily: 10:00am - 6:00pm

November to February:
Daily: 10:00am - 5:00pm

Overview

Year Opened
1704
Owner
Royal Palaces

Signature Cake

The Orangery Cake
£4.50

Afternoon Tea

Signature Orange Tea

Finger sandwiches, orange-scented scone with Cornish clotted cream and strawberry jam, pastries and a choice of teas or coffee.

£15.15

Enchanted Palace Tea

Finger sandwiches, ganache slice and heart-shaped raspberry shortbread, orange-scented scone and a choice of teas or coffee.

£18.35

Royal Champagne Tea

Finger sandwiches, orange-scented scone, éclair, orange and passion fruit tart, a choice of teas or coffee and a glass of Champagne.

£21.00

The Tea Palace English Tea

Sandwiches, mini scones, pastries, a pot of tea and a glass of Champagne.

£34.50

RATING

CAKE
4.25 / 5

OVERALL
4.25 / 5

The Original Maids of Honour

288 Kew Road, TW9 3DU

Open

Mon-Fri.	9:00am - 6:00pm
Sat-Sun.	8:30am - 6:00pm

Overview

Year Opened
1868

Afternoon Tea

Cream Tea

Two plain or fruit scones with clotted cream and jam and a pot of tea.

£6.95 per person

Maids of Honour Afternoon Tea

Two plain or fruit scones with clotted cream and jam, Maids of Honour pastry and a pot of tea.

£9.45 per person

High Tea

Selection of Edwardian tea sandwiches, two plain or fruit scones with clotted cream and jam, Maids of Honour pastry and a pot of tea.

£14.95 per person

Champagne Cream Tea

Half a bottle of Lenoble Brut Reserve French Champagne, bottle of still or sparkling mineral water, chocolate-dipped fresh strawberries, selection of Edwardian sandwiches, two scones with clotted cream, butter and jam, Maids of Honour pastry.

£48.95 for two

enry VIII loved his favourite Maids of Honour tarts so much he locked away the secret recipe. Today this delightful bakery pays tribute to this delicious dessert - pastry tarts filled with lemon-flavoured curd - and continues its tradition of creating melt-in-the-mouth sensations by using only natural and wholesome ingredients. The bakery has been practicing its time-honoured baking skills for the past 120 years, but today, delectable pastries include old favourites such as chocolate éclairs, croissants and custard slice. The bakery also serves traditional English afternoon teas and a selection of refreshments.

Contact

020 8940 2752
www.theoriginalmaidsofhonour.co.uk
manager@theoriginalmaidsofhonour.co.uk

Signature Cake

The Original Maids of Honour Pastry
£2.80

RATING

CAKE
3.50 / 5

OVERALL
3.75 / 5

Ottolenghi Upper Street

287 Upper Street, N1 2TZ

An innovative culinary heaven, Ottolenghi celebrates the glamour and seduction of cakes and desserts. The famous Islington flagship restaurant excels in creating an extensive cake selection that is as visually arresting as it is delicious. Also dealing in savoury fare, everything featured on the menu is made from scratch using fresh ingredients. Ottolenghi's caramel and macadamia cheesecake strikes the perfect balance between creaminess and crunch, while the signature Ottolenghi hot chocolate, made with fresh cream, is testament to the restaurant's refusal to compromise on quality. The interior is lush and modern, with communal tables and clean lines. Customers can dine in or take treats away.

Sister Locations

Notting Hill, Kensington and Belgravia

Signature Cake
Chocolate & Hazlenut Brownie
£2.80

Open

Mon-Sat.	8:00am - 11:00pm
Sun.	9:00am - 7:00pm

Overview

Year Opened
2004
Owner
Yotam Ottolenghi
Pastry Chef
Tomasz Badelek

Suppliers

Tea Supplier
Teapigs
Coffee Supplier
Square Mile Coffee Roasters

Price Range

Coffee & Cake	£5.00+
Cupcakes	£3.20

Contact

020 7288 1454
www.ottolenghi.co.uk
upper@ottolenghi.co.uk

RATING

CAKE
4.75 / 5

OVERALL
4.75 / 5

Flourless Chocolate
Tea cake
£ 4.10 / take away

Outsider Tart

83 Chiswick High Road, W4 2EF

*O*utsider Tart is the story of two New Yorkers who moved to London and found wholesome cupcakes, slices and tarts hard to come by. Drawing on old family recipes, founders David Lesniak and David Muniz turned their favourite hobby - baking - into a business and started Outsider Tart. Upon entry, customers are greeted with an array of generously portioned square slices, cupcakes and cookies laid across a long steel bench featuring a retro rainbow stripe. The menu changes daily, but can include the irresistible Hepburn brownie, Outsider Tart's take on a macadamia and chocolate chip blondie. The texture is creamy and rich, slightly springy on the outside but gooey on the inside. Other delights include the mile high brownie and gluten-free monster slice. Treats are served in novel steel trays. The eclectic interior is designed by owner and architect David Lesniak and features oversized antique circus arrows lined with lights and rustic wooden shelves. American favourites such as Fruit Loops and Hershey's Chocolate are also on display. Excellent service is always on hand.

Sister Locations

Richmond Market and Barnes Market

Signature Cake

Whoopie
Pie
£3.00

Open

Daily:	8:00am - 6:00pm

Overview

Year Opened
2009
Owner
David Muniz & David Lesnak
Pastry Chef
David Muniz & David Lesnak

Suppliers

Tea Supplier
Teapigs
Coffee Supplier
House Peruvian blend

Price Range

Coffee & Cake   £5.50
Cupcakes   £2.35

Contact

020 7096 1609
www.outsidertart.com

CAKE
4.00 / 5

OVERALL
4.25 / 5

RATING

Coffee @ Cake

Coffee & Cake

Patisserie Valerie Marylebone High Street

105 Marylebone High Street, W1U 4RS

Open

Mon-Fri.	7:30am - 6:00pm
Sat.	8:00am - 7:00pm
Sun.	8:30am - 6:00pm

Overview

Year Opened
1993
Owner
Patisserie Holdings Ltd
Pastry Chef
Luis Riveiro

Suppliers

Tea Supplier
Algerian Coffee
Coffee Supplier
Illy

Price Range

Coffee & Cake	£4.45 - £6.90
Cupcakes	£2.35

*T*his haven of indulgent handmade delights was founded by Belgian-born Madam Valerie in 1926. Today a British institution, Patisserie Valerie continues to offer delicious cakes, gateaux and pastries. Among its most popular choices is the apple tart, a butter pastry with an apple, sultana and cinnamon filling topped with sliced apples and an apricot glaze. The mixed berry mousse is also a highlight and is comprised of a vanilla sponge base topped with layers of whipped cream mousse, berry glaze and fresh fruit. European in feel, the front window and inside counter is lined with sweet treats. Customers can enjoy desserts amid the opulent setting, which features prettily painted walls and decadent archways. A selection of teas and coffees accompanies the cakes.

Afternoon Tea

Madame Valerie Cream Tea

Two scones with a choice of toppings
and a pot of tea.

£6.25

Signature Cake

Double Chocolate
Gateau
£3.95

Contact

020 7935 6240
www.patisserie-valerie.co.uk
marylebone@valeriecafe.co.uk

Sister Locations

33 locations around the UK

CAKE
3.75 / 5

OVERALL
4.00 / 5

★★★★☆

Paul Baker Street
Unit 65, 55 Baker Street, W1U 8EW

For those looking for a grand French bakery experience, Paul is a perfect tea-time treat. Cake lovers can step into the spacious Baker Street store and enjoy the tarts, éclairs, croissants and pastries on offer. The front counter sparkles with delectable delights including vibrantly coloured oversized macarons and Paul's best-selling lemon tarts. An array of artisanal breads and tempting Viennoiserie pastries complete the selection. The opulent setting has a fittingly French style and features debonair chequered floors, antique chandeliers and mirrors. A selection of coffee, hot chocolate and tea is also available.

Contact
020 7486 0626
www.paul-uk.com

Sister Locations
28 London locations

Open

Mon-Fri.	7.00am - 7.00pm
Sat.	8.00am - 6.00pm
Sun.	9.00am - 5.00pm

Overview
Year Opened
2006
Owner
Francis Holder

Suppliers
Coffee Supplier
Lavazza

Price Range
Coffee & Cake   £5.60 - £6.90

Signature Cake
Grand Macaron
£3.60

RATING

CAKE
4.00 / 5

OVERALL
4.25 / 5

Peggy Porschen Parlour

*F*ounded by award-winning cake designer Peggy Porschen, this Belgravia-based cake parlour offers exquisite miniature cakes, cupcakes, muffins and cookies. Delights are made and decorated on site by master bakers, pâtissiers and sugar artists and each creation is a work of art, to look at and to taste. Cupcake flavours include sticky toffee and black forest and low-calorie muffins have proved popular with yummy mummies. Exclusive blends of loose leaf tea complement the cupcakes. Housed in a bubblegum pink Georgian-style building, the cake shop's ambiance is intimate, with enchanting designs featured throughout the café. The Parlour also sells Peggy's homewares and cake accessories, but it's her cakes that make this experience so exceptional.

Signature Cake

Cupcakes
£3.50

116 Ebury Street, SW1W 9QQ

Open

| Mon-Sat. | 9:00am - 6:00pm |
| Sun. | 10:00am - 6:00pm |

Overview

Year Opened
2003
Owner
Peggy Porschen & Bryn Morrow
Pastry Chef
Cinthia Panariello

Suppliers

Tea Supplier
Blends for Friends
Coffee Supplier
Illy

Price Range

| Coffee & Cake | £6.00 |
| Cupcakes | £3.50 |

Contact

020 7730 1316
www.peggyporschen.com
info@peggyporschen.com

RATING

CAKE
4.25 / 5

OVERALL
4.25 / 5 ★★★★⯪

Petersham Nurseries

Church Lane, TW10 7AG

*S*erving coffee and cake with a twist, Petersham Nurseries Café is set in a charming greenhouse featuring eclectic furniture, hessian walls and wrought-iron tables. Michelin-starred chef and food writer Skye Gyngell creates a gastronomic adventure for her clientele using the seasonal produce growing in the kitchen garden of Petersham House - particularly its wide range of herbs and fruit. Afternoon tea is comprised of delicious homemade cakes, biscuits, ice creams, whole leaf teas and English fruit juices, and tea-tasting workshops are also available. Delectable dessert options include steamed pudding with ginger, blackberries and double cream, and hazelnut panna cotta with caramel.

Open

Mon.	Closed
Tues-Sat.	12:00am - 3:00pm
Sun.	12:00am - 3:30pm

Overview

Year Opened
2004
Owner
Gael & Francesco Boglione
Pastry Chef
Skye Gyngell

Suppliers

Tea Supplier
Canton Tea Company
Coffee Supplier
Allpress

Price Range

Coffee & Cake   £11.00

Contact

020 8605 3627
www.petershamnurseries.com
info@petershamnurseries.com

Signature Cake

Orange & Almond Cake
£8.00

CAKE
4.00 / 5

OVERALL
4.25 / 5

RATING

Peyton & Byrne St Pancras

Unit 11, The Undercroft, St. Pancras International, NW1 2QP

*R*enowned for its superb range of cakes, tarts, biscuits and buns, Peyton and Byrne celebrates classic British home baking. Cake lovers are treated to a magnificent array of luxurious delights beautifully displayed in the St Pancras store's floor-to-ceiling glass windows. Decadent layer cakes, colourful cupcakes and mouth-watering fairy cakes are moist in texture and boast luscious toppings. Crowd favourites include the frou frou butterfly cake – a luxurious creation that balances sweet coconut with tart raspberries. Guests can sit and enjoy treats amid the modern stainless steel furniture, extravagant feature arches and a mint green colour scheme. Creations on offer are seasonally inspired and savoury fare is also available.

Open

Daily: 7:30am - 8:00pm

Overview

Year Opened
2008
Owner
Oliver Peyton

Suppliers

Tea Supplier
Sri Lanka Tea and various others
Coffee Supplier
L'Unico and Peyton & Byrne

Price Range

Coffee & Cake £4.30 - £4.60
Cupcakes £2.30 - £2.40

Contact

020 7278 6707
www.peytonandbyrne.co.uk
st.pancras@peytonandbyrne.co.uk

Signature Cake
Victoria Sponge
£2.20

RATING
CAKE
4.50 / 5

OVERALL
3.75 / 5

Princi

135 Wardour Street, W1F 0UT

*T*his buzzing Soho branch of the Milanese boutique bakery radiates excitement, allure and charm. Customers are presented with tray upon tray of gastronomic delights including a spectrum of savoury pizzas, salads and breads, as well as seemingly endless cakes, tarts, pastries and slices. Sweet creations include sfogliatelle, brownies, croissants and a signature passion fruit cheesecake. Catering for all phases of the evening, Princi is a popular choice for after-work drinks, dinner or sweet treats. The suave stone and marble splashback within creates a feel of modern elegance. A multitude of tables are available to those lucky enough to spot a space, but remember, Princi offers counter service only.

Contact

020 7478 8888
www.princi.co.uk
info@princi.co.uk

 Find Princi's Tiramisu recipe on page 157

Open

| Mon-Sat. | 7:00am - 12:00am |
| Sun. | 9:00am - 10:00pm |

Overview

Year Opened
2008
Owner
Rocco Princi & Alan Yau
Pastry Chef
Max Porta

Suppliers

Tea Supplier
Drury
Coffee Supplier
Monmouth

Signature Cake
Passion Fruit Cheesecake
£4.60

Price Range

Coffee & Cake   £4.20 - £6.80

RATING

CAKE
4.50 / 5

OVERALL
4.75 / 5

Sweet Desserts

64 Exmouth Market, EC1R 4QP

Pear & Almond Tart · Apple Tart · Chocolate Tart

Sweet Baked Lemon Tart · Sweet Baby Cup

This French-inspired boulangerie and pâtisserie delights cake lovers with a delectable range of mouth-watering creations. Rows of perfectly presented desserts resemble edible works of art and offerings include rich chocolate and fruit tarts, delicious chocolate brownies and creamy éclairs. Set in the Exmouth Market culinary precinct, this classy bakery uses premium ingredients to create fine desserts. Once a derelict property, the interior has been converted into a sleek eatery with a polished wood theme and stainless steel splashback. The popular Sweet Desserts also has a stall at Borough Market.

Contact

020 7713 6777
www.sweetdesserts.co.uk
info@sweetdesserts.co.uk

Sister Locations

Borough Market stall

Open

Daily:	7:00am - 6:30pm

Overview

Year Opened
2003
Owner
Eddy Grappy
Pastry Chef
Justice Ohene Kwame

Suppliers

Tea Supplier
Locally sourced
Coffee Supplier
Nude

Signature Cake
Canele de Bordeaux
£1.30

Price Range

Coffee & Cake   £3.60+

RATING

CAKE
4.00 / 5

OVERALL
3.75 / 5

Violet
47 Wilton Way, E8 3ED

*T*ucked away on the serene Wilton Way, Violet is a popular East London hangout that serves American-style cupcakes, whoopie pies and other treats. Customers are greeted with an array of sweet-smelling delights within a small but warm and comforting cottage space. Founder Claire Ptaz is often on hand and is happy to let customers watch her create. Among favourites are signature specials, the ginger molasses cake and salted caramel cupcake. Violet's bite-sized cupcakes, another delicious option, are easy on both the waist and wallet. On a fine day customers can enjoy the British sun on the back terrace or in a more spacious dining area upstairs. Perfect for an intimate catch-up, this favourite also serves excellent coffee.

Sister Locations
Broadway Market and Maltby Street Market

Signature Cake

Ginger Molasses
Cake
£2.50

Find Violet's Chocolate Chip Whoopie Pie recipe on page 151

Open

Mon.	Closed
Tues-Fri.	8:00am - 6:00pm
Sat.	10:00am - 6:00pm
Sun.	10:00am - 5:00pm

Overview

Year Opened
2010
Owner
Claire Ptak

Suppliers

Tea Supplier
MayKingTea
Coffee Supplier
Coleman & Square Mile Coffee Roasters

Price Range

| Coffee & Cake | £5.00 |
| Cupcakes | £0.90 - £2.80 |

Contact

020 7275 8360
www.violetcakes.com
info@violetcakes.com

RATING

CAKE
4.50 / 5

OVERALL
4.25 / 5

Yauatcha

15 Broadwick Street, W1F 0DL

This energetic Michelin-starred dim sum teahouse also offers a sophisticated range of carefully crafted sweet treats. Specialty teas and coffees are available to accompany the collection of decadent desserts, handmade macarons (including sesame and pandan flavours) and chocolates. The pristinely presented chocolate raspberry delice balances a delectable creamy raspberry chocolate mousse with a rich dark chocolate brownie base and is topped with vanilla bean ice cream. The buzzing ground-floor dining room fuses traditional Chinese teahouse features with electric blue bursts and modern design. Perfect for a special occasion, Yauatcha is unpretentious yet stylish.

Open

Mon-Sat.	12:00pm - 11.45pm
Sun.	12:00pm - 10.30pm

Overview

Year Opened
2004
Owner
Tasameen Ltd
Pastry Chef
Sarah Barber

Suppliers

Tea Supplier
Master Kung
Coffee Supplier
Kontra Musetti

Price Range

Coffee & Cake   £4.00 - £10.50

Contact

020 7494 8888
www.yauatcha.com
reservations@yauatcha.com

Signature Cake

Macarons
£1.50

Find Yauatcha's Vanilla Macaroon recipe on page 158

 CAKE
4.75 / 5

 OVERALL
4.75 / 5

RATING

Afternoon Tea

Afternoon Tea History & Etiquette

Afternoon Tea or High Tea?

It is a common misconception that afternoon tea and high tea are the same thing, but in fact, each meal has its own distinct origins and practices. The "high" in high tea is not an indicator of class, but instead describes the type of table the meal was originally eaten on. High tea was a term used to describe a working class supper consisting of meat and fish dishes, baked goods and vegetables. The large servings of food required that high tea be eaten on a formal, or "high", dining table. Conversely, "low tea" was a term for the afternoon tea traditionally eaten by wealthy ladies during the 19th century. The meal was served in sitting rooms on occasional tables, which were both smaller in size and lower to the ground. Although initially an informal meal enjoyed alone or with a few friends, the rituals and etiquette surrounding afternoon tea were soon developed and embellished by the gentry and exported around the world. Although the practices of low and high tea have since become more or less the same, the modern high tea – a selection of sweets and savouries served with a pot of fine tea – has become a popular treat at London's finest hotels.

The Origins of Afternoon Tea

The practice of drinking tea in England became common following the marriage of King Charles II to the Portuguese princess Catherine of Braganza in 1662. Following exploration and the development of trade in the Far East, tea became popular at the Portuguese court but remained extremely rare in London. After arriving in England, Catherine soon became a trendsetter at the English court and her preference for tea saw it become extremely fashionable in aristocratic circles.

The development of afternoon tea as a social gathering is attributed to Anna Maria Stanhope, the seventh Duchess of Bedford, in the early 1840s. Before the mid-1800s, only two meals were eaten each day, but as gas and oil lights were introduced into the homes of the wealthy, the second meal, usually eaten before dark, was eaten later and later. This created the need for a light midday snack (the origin of today's lunch), but the Duchess found this was not enough to keep her hunger at bay until the evening. Said to suffer from "a sinking feeling" by late afternoon, Anna had her servants secretly serve her small meals consisting of bread, butter, cake and tea in her boudoir. She so enjoyed this refreshment that she soon began to invite her close friends to join her for "afternoon tea". To the Duchess' surprise, her indulgence became increasingly popular, so she chose to continue it upon her return to London, where other hostesses also adopted the practice.

Following the French colonisation of Morocco, tea dances became popular both in the Royal Navy and as a continuation of garden parties. More modest than a ball, a tea dance saw refreshments such as tea and coffee, ices, champagne-cup and claret-cup, fruit, sandwiches, cake and biscuits displayed as a buffet in the dining room, while an orchestra played waltzes, tangos and later the Charleston. These dances traditionally took place in the palm court of prestigious hotels and, to this day, afternoon tea is served in these rooms in many hotels, including The Ritz and The Langham.

Afternoon Tea Etiquette

Making tea

Tea should be brewed for two to four minutes, depending on the type of tea. The correct amount is roughly one rounded teaspoon of loose tea per cup.

The addition of milk before or after the pouring of the tea is a matter of debate. In Victorian tradition, pouring tea straight into the cup was a test of the quality of porcelain, as only the most expensive bone china could withstand the heat of the tea without cracking. These days, tea purists pour milk into the cup first, as adding milk into hot tea makes denaturation of milk proteins more likely and can damage the flavour of the tea. By pouring the milk into the teacup first and adding the tea second, the whole beverage will be slightly cooler but more fragrant to taste.

Teacups should be filled to below the brim to allow room for milk to be added and reduce the likelihood of the tea being spilled into the saucer. Once the tea is poured, it should go straight to the recipient to avoid becoming too cool.

Lemon should be added to tea in slices, not wedges, and should never be used with milk. Lemon should be added after the tea has been poured and a lemon fork should be provided.

Tea should be stirred without the spoon clinking against the china and, after stirring, the spoon should be placed gently on the saucer in line with the handle of the teacup, in approximately the four o'clock position.

Drinking Tea

Perhaps the most contentious issue of tea etiquette is the arching or raising of the little finger when holding a teacup. There are a variety of theories as to why this habit came about; some say it was necessitated by the first teacups to arrive from China, which had no handles. These cups were held with the thumbs and fingers in the six and 12 o'clock positions, which required the little fingers to be raised for extra balance. A more practical reason is that raising or arching the little finger prevents it from being burned by the base of the teacup. An arched pinky also allows more control when placing a teacup back into its saucer, thereby reducing noise and the chance of spills. Currently, the propriety of the raised or arched little finger remains a matter of debate, but many see it as a considerate practice that often prevents spills.

The teacup should be held with the index finger through the handle, but not looped around it. The thumb should rest on top and the middle finger below the handle for balance, with the last two fingers curled. Alternatively, the handle can be lightly pinched, with the other hand taking the weight of the cup, without cradling it.

When drinking tea, it is appropriate to lower your eyes to guide the cup to your mouth, then to sip delicately without slurping. If at a table, the saucer should not be lifted, but when appropriate, it should rest on the four fingers of the left hand with the teacup held in the right (unless the user is left-handed).

∞∞∞∞∞∞∞

Eating

Napkins

Napkins should always be provided and used. They should be picked up gently, without flourish or flapping, after the host has done so but before the food arrives. Napkins should rest on the lap and be folded to fit if necessary, with the fold facing towards the body. Gentle dabbing at the mouth is best and napkins should not be used as a handkerchief (except in emergencies or to catch an unexpected sneeze), nor to blot lipstick or mop up spills, as these stains can be difficult to remove.

When leaving the table in the middle of tea, the napkin should be loosely placed on the chair and the chair tucked into the table. Of course, if the napkin is dirty, be wary of soiling the chair; if necessary, it is best to avoid this by placing the napkin on the table as a cloth is more easily laundered than a chair cover. Only upon completion of tea should the napkin be placed back on the table on the left-hand side of the place setting.

Place Settings and Cutlery

When unsure about which utensil to use, work your way from the outside of the place setting to the inside. While a petite knife and fork may be used together for an open sandwich, it is preferable that these utensils are not used together on a closed sandwich. However, due to the evolving nature of the foods presently served for afternoon tea, this may not always be the case.

Sandwiches

The meal should not be started until all guests are at the table and the food from each course has been served.

Traditionally, savoury sandwiches are eaten first, but scones are also often eaten while still warm. This means that they may be placed at the top of an afternoon tea stand to allow the addition of a cover for insulation.

Sandwiches should be of an appropriate size so that three fingers are all that is needed to lift them. In some circles, crusts are removed from sandwiches, but as long as they can be easily eaten, there is no reason to cut off crusts if you prefer otherwise.

Food should always be tasted before it is seasoned with salt and pepper as adding it first can be impolite to the cook. The mouth should of course be kept closed when eating and only small bites taken to allow conversation to continue unimpeded.

Scones

While many assume that to slice a scone horizontally and cover it in jam and clotted cream is acceptable, this action is actually considered improper tea etiquette as it can be messy to prepare and to eat. The correct method is the same as for the dinner roll: a small piece should be broken off and individually spread with jam and cream.

No guests should reach across the table to pick up shared food items such as clotted cream or preserves, and should ask for them to be passed around the table upon request. When an item has been requested, those passing it along should not help themselves to the item first. Cream or jam should be placed on individual plates with a small serving spoon, then spread on the scones using individual knives.

Whether jam or cream is added first depends on preference for the Devonshire (cream first) or Cornish (jam first) tradition.

Pastries

Afternoon tea is fundamentally a ladylike affair, but it can often be difficult to maintain propriety due to the mess that often results from eating cakes. Depending on the type of cake, there are different table manners on how to eat it. Fingers should be used for dry and crumbly cakes such as cupcakes, while moist cake should be eaten with a fork. Petits fours can be eaten with the fingers or with a fork if they are larger than a few bites.

The Berkeley
Wilton Place, SW1X 7RL

*D*rawing inspiration from London's glittering fashion scene, Prêt-à-Portea at the Berkeley presents pastries modelled from dazzling designer items. Creating delicious desserts replicating handbags and dresses, each creation is a work of art. The real treat however is devouring them. Fashionistas can feast on the exquisite chocolate Chloé praline clutch or the light and fruity Tory Burch bavarois. Making for a special experience, canapés, sandwiches and cakes are served on china designed by Paul Smith. The original selections of teas include unique blends such as the pear caramel. Sprinkled with a smattering of special touches, afternoon tea takers are treated to their own personal name card, friendly service and a handbag takeaway box for unfinished goodies.

Overview
Year Opened
1901
Owner
Maybourne Hotel Group
Restaurant Name
The Caramel Room
Pastry Chef
Mourad Khiat

Open
Daily, seatings every half hour between 1:00pm and 5:30pm

Afternoon Tea
Prêt-à-Portea
Selection of sandwiches,canapés, designer-inspired pastries and coffee or loose leaf tea.
£37.50

Champagne Prêt-à-Portea
The Prêt-à-Portea Afternoon Tea accompanied by a glass of Laurent-Perrier Champagne.
£47.50

Couture Champagne Prêt-à-Portea
The Prêt-à-Portea Afternoon Tea accompanied by a glass of Billecart-Salmon Rosé, Laurent Perrier Ultra Brut or Laurent Perrier Grand Siècle.
£54.50

Contact
020 7107 8866
www.the-berkeley.co.uk
dining@the-berkeley.co.uk

RATING

CAKE
4.75 / 5

OVERALL
4.50 / 5

Image supplied by The Berkeley

The Chesterfield Mayfair

35 Charles Street, W1J 5EB

Image supplied by The Chesterfield Mayfair

*L*ocated in the heart of Mayfair, this hidden jewel bursts with English charm. The light airy conservatory is reminiscent of an elegant secret garden. Traditional afternoon teas are on offer - with or without a splash of Champagne. Chocolate lovers can indulge in the Chocolate Lover's Tea, a sensational feast which includes melty chocolate scones. The flowering teas are exquisite, with a lovely aroma and flavour. Unlimited refreshments are also at hand. Attentive waiters will ensure your experience is a special one. The Chesterfield Mayfair is the perfect place to meet family and friends, and the children's afternoon tea further confirms the conservatory as a delightful culinary haven with something for everyone.

Overview

Year Opened
1973

Owner
Red Carnation Hotels

Restaurant Name
Butlers Restaurant, The Conservatory

Pastry Chef
Tom Coleman

Suppliers

Tea Supplier
Twinings

Coffee Supplier
Starbucks

Open

Daily, seatings every 15 minutes
between 1:30pm and 5:15pm

Afternoon Tea

The Chesterfield Traditional Afternoon Tea

Homemade sandwiches, freshly baked homemade scones with clotted cream and preserve, a selection of pastries, cupcakes and a range of teas.

£25.50

The Chocolate Lover's Tea

Sandwiches, freshly baked chocolate scones, a selection of chocolate pastries and cupcakes, accompanied by hot chocolate or a chocolate milkshake.

£27.50

Little Prince and Princess Afternoon Tea

Peanut butter and jam sandwiches, a cupcake, ice cream and a milkshake or soft drink.

£11.50

The Chesterfield Champagne Tea

The Chesterfield Traditional Afternoon Tea with a glass of Taittinger Brut or Demi-Sec Champagne.

£33.50 / £36.50

Contact

020 7491 2622
www.chesterfieldmayfair.com

RATING

CAKE
4.00 / 5

OVERALL
4.00 / 5

Claridge's

49 Brook Street, W1K 4HR

Image supplied by Claridge's

 Open

Daily, seatings at 3:00pm, 3:30pm,
5.00pm and 5:30pm

Afternoon Tea

Afternoon Tea

Selection of wafer-thin sandwiches, freshly
baked scones with Marco Polo jelly (Claridge's
own tea-infused jam) and Devonshire cream,
assorted teacakes and pastries and a choice of
tea or coffee.

£38.00

Champagne Afternoon Tea

Traditional Afternoon Tea accompanied by a
glass of selected Champagne.

£49.00

Rosé Champagne Afternoon Tea

Traditional Afternoon Tea accompanied by a
glass of selected Rosé Champagne.

£62.00

Seasonal Afternoon Tea

For the Holiday Season, Valentine's Day and
Mother's Day.

£55.00

Contact

020 7107 8872
www.claridges.co.uk
dining@claridges.co.uk

---

*T*he 2011 winner of the Tea Guild's Best
London Afternoon Tea award, Claridge's is a
grand venue, featuring beautiful art deco
embellishment. The afternoon tea is a
scrumptious English feast of scones, pastries
and savouries. The cakes and pastries are
masterpieces and the Marco Polo jelly - jam
infused with the hotel's specialty tea blend -
the perfect accompaniment to lovely light
scones. Amazing assortments of over 30 teas
are served in delicate striped china and each
table enjoys a three-tier trolley of treats.
Champagne afternoon teas are also available.
The surroundings are luxurious and the
opulent interior is tastefully decorated in hues
of green and cream.

Overview

Year Opened
1856
Owner
Maybourne Hotel Group
Restaurant Name
The Foyer and Reading Room
Pastry Chef
Nick Patterson

Suppliers

Tea Supplier
L'Unico
Coffee Supplier
Nespresso

RATING

CAKE
4.00 / 5

OVERALL
4.50 / 5

Fortnum & Mason

181 Piccadilly, W1A 1ER

From an iconic British institution such as Fortnum & Mason, one would expect nothing less than a truly delightful afternoon tea – and the St. James's Restaurant delivers everything expected and more. Afternoon tea lovers can relax in armchairs while snappily dressed wait-staff deliver canapés, cakes, biscuits and scones. The venue is formal yet tranquil, with gentle piano music floating through the air. The afternoon tea experience commences with a selection of warm canapés, followed by sandwiches, scones and cakes. An impressive selection of tea accompanies. Scones are served with a selection of Fortnum's preserves and clotted cream and the large tray of cakes ensures everyone is treated to sweets they will adore. The restaurant also caters for children, and for those with special dietary requirements if arranged in advance.

Overview

Year Opened
1707
Owner
Wittington Investments Ltd
Restaurant Name
St. James's Restaurant

Suppliers

Tea Supplier
Various

Contact

0845 602 5694
www.fortnumandmason.com

Open

Daily, seatings any time between:
Mon-Sat.   12:00pm - 6:30pm
Sun.   12:00pm - 4:30pm

Afternoon Tea

Fortnum's Classic Afternoon Tea

Selection of canapés, finger sandwiches, warm scones with a choice of Fortnum & Mason preserves, a choice of cakes and a Fortnum's Classic Blend Tea.

£34.00

Fortnum's Estate Afternoon Tea

The Fortnum's Classic Afternoon Tea with a choice of Fortnum's Single Estate Tea.

£38.00

Gluten-Free Afternoon Tea

A gluten-free version of the The Fortnum's Classic Afternoon Tea with Fortnum's Classic Blend Tea.

£34.00

Fortnum's High Tea

Selection of canapés, choice of one savoury dish, scones with Fortnum & Mason preserves, selection of cakes and Fortnum's Classic Blend Tea.

£36.00

Children's Afternoon Tea

For 4-10 year olds, it includes a selection of canapés, finger sandwiches, scones, a raspberry jam biscuit, tea cakes and Fortnum's Classic Blend Tea, hot chocolate or fruit juice.

£17.00

RATING

CAKE
4.25 / 5

OVERALL
4.50 / 5

Grosvenor House

Park Lane, W1K 7TN

Image supplied by Grosvenor House

Open

Daily, seatings at:

Mon-Fri.	2:00pm, 2:30pm, 4:00pm and 4:30pm
Sat-Sun.	Every half hour between 1:00pm and 5:00pm

The elegant Park Room is a momentous afternoon tea treat. A quintessential British experience, dining at the historic Grosvenor House has proved popular among royalty and celebrities since opening in the 1920s. Guests can enjoy afternoon tea in the Park Room, which boasts floor-to-ceiling windows with views of Hyde Park, delicate place settings and soft piano music. Afternoon tea options are plentiful and children are invited to attend Grover's Tea Time where they will receive a take-home Grover toy. A gluten-free afternoon tea option is also available. There is no strict dress code, although most dress to impress.

Overview

Year Opened
1929
Owner
J W Marriott
Restaurant Name
The Park Room and Library
Pastry Chef
Nigel Bruschetti

Suppliers

Tea Supplier
Twinings
Coffee Supplier
Illy

Contact

020 7399 8452
www.parkroom.co.uk
mhrs.longh.park.room@marriotthotels.com

Afternoon Tea

Anna's Tea

Named after the seventh Duchess of Bedford who is credited with the introduction of afternoon tea into British tradition, this tea includes a selection of finger sandwiches, scones, cream puffs and French pastries, and a selection of teas.

£32.50

Hendrick's Tea Time

Selection of finger sandwiches, scones with Devonshire clotted cream and Cornish strawberry jam, cream puffs, French pastries, a choice of tea and a Hendrick's Martini.

£43.00

Grover's Tea Time

Tropical fruit salad, ice cream, a French pastry, a glass of non-alcoholic Luscombe Wild Elderflower Bubbly and a soft Grover toy.

£11.50

West Country Cream Tea

Scones, Cornish strawberry jam, comb honey and Devonshire clotted cream, and a choice of tea.

£17.00

RATING

CAKE
4.00 / 5

OVERALL
4.25 / 5

The Landmark

222 Marylebone Street, NW1 6JQ

Image supplied by The Landmark

The Landmark's striking Winter Garden restaurant is set in a luxurious eight-storey atrium showcasing an impressive glass roof and a fresh outdoor ambiance. Finger sandwiches and scones are freshly made with detail and care. The pastries are presented with flair - look out for the Pimm's jelly with fresh strawberries. The very special Chocolate Afternoon Tea offers melt-in-the-mouth delights including chocolate scones. Delicious gluten-free treats including fruit tartlets, sorbet lollipops and cheesecakes are also available. The traditional afternoon tea menu changes seasonally.

Overview

Year Opened
1899
Owner
The Lancaster Landmark Hotel Company
Restaurant Name
The Winter Garden
Pastry Chef
Ammar Khliel

Suppliers

Tea Supplier
Tea Palace
Coffee Supplier
Illy

Open

Daily, seatings any time between:
Mon-Fri. 3:00pm - 6:00pm
Sat-Sun. 2:30pm - 6:30pm

Afternoon Tea

The Winter Garden Afternoon Tea

Selection of sandwiches, freshly baked scones with Cornish clotted cream and homemade strawberry preserve, French seasonally inspired pastries and a selection of teas.

£40.00

Chocolate Afternoon Tea

Finger sandwiches, pastries, freshly baked chocolate chip or fruit peel scones, chocolate delights including chocolate and raspberry crème brûlée, baked white chocolate cheesecake and chocolate-dipped strawberries.

£42.00

Afternoon Tea with Champagne

The Winter Garden Afternoon Tea or Chocolate Afternoon Tea with a glass of Taittinger Champagne or Taittinger Rosé.

£45.00 / £50.00

Gluten-Free Afternoon Tea

Gluten-free sandwiches, freshly baked scones, pastries, macarons, fruit tartlets, meringue, crème brûlée and a sorbet lollipop.

£42.00

Contact

020 7631 8000
www.wintergarden-london.com
restaurants.reservation@thelandmark.co.uk

RATING

CAKE
4.50 / 5

OVERALL ★ ★ ★ ★ ⯪
4.50 / 5

The Langham

1c Portland Place, Regent Street, W1B 1JA

The Langham was one of the first hotels in London to serve afternoon tea when it opened in 1865. After an extensive refurbishment in 2009, this tradition returned with a vengeance, and the establishment won the Tea Guild's Top London Afternoon Tea Award in 2010. In earlier times, Sherlock Holmes author Sir Arthur Conan Doyle was one of many celebrities to frequent the venue. Although much has changed since its initial opening, The Langham remains popular among its prestigious regulars. The opulent room features jewelled gates at the entrance, lashings of gold detailing across the walls, high ceilings and a grand piano. For those after a traditional offering, the Wonderland Tea includes richly flavoured sandwiches, warm scones and pastries. Inspired by a jewellery collection, the decadent Bijoux Tea has open sandwiches featuring luxurious delicacies such as quail's breast, lobster or foie gras, and pastries. High Tea and the 1865 Langham High Tea are also available. Diligent service ensures tea is topped up and treats are served regularly. The Langham is the perfect venue for a memorable celebration or special occasion and offers one of the best afternoon tea experiences in London.

Overview

Year Opened
1865
Owner
Langham Hotels International
Restaurant Name
Palm Court
Pastry Chef
Cherish Finden

Contact

020 7965 0195
www.palm-court.co.uk
reservations@palm-court.co.uk

Open

Daily, seatings at 1:00pm, 3:15pm and 5:30pm

Afternoon Tea

Wonderland Afternoon Tea

Finger sandwiches, a selection of plain and golden raisin scones with clotted cream and strawberry preserve, a selection of French pastries, mini cakes including a Valrhona chocolate tower and a choice of teas.

£38.00

Stephen Webster Bijoux Afternoon Tea

Open sandwiches, raisin and chocolate scones, a selection of statement pastries and a choice of teas.

£49.00

Champagne Wonderland Afternoon Tea

The Wonderland Afternoon Tea with a glass of Laurent-Perrier Brut Reserve.

£50.00

Champagne Bijoux Afternoon Tea

The Bijoux Afternoon tea with a glass of Louis Roederer Brut Premier or Laurent Perrier Brut Reserve.

£63.00

Über Bijoux Afternoon Tea for Two

Bijoux Afternoon Tea for two with a half bottle of Laurent Perrier Brut Reserve.

£122.00

CAKE 4.75 / 5

OVERALL 4.75 / 5

Image supplied by The Langham

Le Méridien Piccadilly

21 Piccadilly, W1J OBH

Image supplied by Le Méridien Piccadilly

Open

Daily, seatings any time between
12:00pm and 6:00pm

Afternoon Tea

The Terrace Afternoon Tea

Selection of finger sandwiches, homemade
scones with strawberry jam and clotted cream,
French pastries, a choice of tea or coffee.

£25.00

Le Méridien Champagne Afternoon Tea

The Terrace Afternoon Tea with a glass
of champagne.

£35.00

Light Tea

Scones with strawberry jam and clotted
cream, French pastries and a choice of
tea or coffee.

£18.00

*R*elax and enjoy afternoon tea in
elegance and style at The Terrace Restaurant.
Set in the heart of London, the restaurant's
contemporary edge and French flair create a
sanctuary of calm. Glass ceilings and walls
create a light and airy feel. Served on stylish
slate cake stands, treats include dainty finger
sandwiches, warm homemade scones and
delicate French pastries. The extensive
Twinings tea selection includes a popular
blackcurrant and lavender blend. Those
seeking something different can look to the
Yerba Mate blend, featuring smoky overtones
and a dry finish.

Overview

Year Opened
1974
Restaurant Name
The Terrace Restaurant
Pastry Chef
Lisa Mansel

Suppliers

Tea Supplier
Twinings
Coffee Supplier
Illy

Contact

020 7851 3085
www.terracerestaurantlondon.co.uk
piccadilly.terrace@lemeridien.com

RATING

CAKE
4.00 / 5

OVERALL
4.00 / 5

The Mandeville Hotel

Mandeville Place, W1U 2BE

Open

Daily, seatings any time between:
Mon-Fri.   3:00pm - 5:00pm,
Sat-Sun.   1:00pm - 5:00pm

Afternoon Tea

Fashion Tea Menu

Traditional English sandwiches, freshly baked scones, pastries and cakes including designer cupcakes, pink meringues and Mandeville Macaroons. An extensive selection of teas are available. Champagne can be enjoyed for an additional cost.

£26.50

Men's Tea

Sandwiches including a mini cheeseburger and steak and shallot jam sandwich; traditional scones, a range of desserts such as basil panna cotta. A range of teas are on offer. Whisky or Champagne are available for an additional cost.

£26.50

*O*ffering a sophisticated afternoon tea experience to ladies and gents, The Mandeville Hotel has something for everyone. In an update on the English tradition, men are invited to relax and unwind over a Men's Afternoon Tea, which features more masculine fare such as roast sirloin sandwiches, mini cheeseburgers, basil pana cotta and whisky. Consumed over a round of backgammon, the Men's Afternoon Tea is also available for ladies. Also worthy of special mention is the Fashion Ladies Afternoon Tea, which offers sandwiches, pink meringues and designer cupcakes presented on Royal Doulton china designed by Zandra Rhodes.

Overview

Year Opened
1982
Restaurant Name
The deVille Restaurant
Pastry Chef
Bruce Marais

Suppliers

Tea Supplier
Jing Tea
Coffee Supplier
Musetti

Contact

020 7935 5599
www.mandeville.co.uk
info@mandeville.co.uk

RATING

CAKE
4.25 / 5

OVERALL
4.00 / 5

Millennium Hotel London Mayfair

44 Grosvenor Square, W1K 2HP

Open

Daily, seatings any time between
3:00pm and 5:30pm

*Incredibly good value, this afternoon tea option is located in luxury five-star hotel surroundings. Set in The Pine Bar, this dining experience is a fabulous option for those on a budget. Indulge in the range of high-quality teas, elegant sandwiches, delicious scones and a delicate selection of pastries. The perfectly brewed teas come with a colour-coded personal timer and service is with a smile.

Overview

Year Opened
1996
Owner
Millenium & Copthorne Hotels
Restaurant Name
Pine Bar
Pastry Chef
Peter Sawbridge

Suppliers

Tea Supplier
Twinings
Coffee Supplier
Douwe Egberts

Afternoon Tea

Traditional Cream Tea

Warm baked sultana scones with Devonshire clotted cream and preserves, and a pot of tea.

£10.50

The Mayfair Full Afternoon Tea

Selection of homemade sandwiches, warm baked sultana scones with devonshire clotted cream and preserves, homemade pastries and a pot of tea.

£15.50

The Mayfair Celebration Tea

The Mayfair Full Afternoon Tea with a glass of champagne.

£35.00

Contact

020 7629 9400
www.millenniumhotels.co.uk
goran.dzatev@millenniumhotels.co.uk

RATING

CAKE
4.00 / 5

OVERALL
4.00 / 5

Park Lane Hotel

Piccadilly, W1J 7BX

Image supplied by Park Lane Hotel

Open

Daily, seatings any time between
3:00pm and 5:30pm

Afternoon Tea

The Park Lane Afternoon Tea

Selection of finger sandwiches, scones with
clotted cream and seasonal preserve, French
pastries, a choice of teas and a glass of
Taittinger Brut Prestige Rose Champagne.

£32.00

Varied Seasonal Afternoon Tea

Selection of seasonal savouries, plain scones
with clotted Devonshire cream and fruit
preserve, selectional seasonal cakes and
pastries and a choice of loose teas.

£42.00

Art Deco Afternoon Tea

Selection of finger sandwiches, scones with
clotted cream and seasonal preserve, French
pastries, a choice of tea and a glass of Mumm
Special Brut Champagne.

£38.00

Contact

020 7290 7328
www.palmcourtlondon.co.uk
palmcourt.parklane@sheraton.com

This art deco gem features a stunning
stained-glass ceiling that brings dappled light
into the green and gold room. The variety of
afternoon tea options all deliver a luxurious
experience that will transport diners back to
the Jazz Age. For those after something
different, the Autumn Afternoon Tea includes a
passion fruit meringue trifle. Exquisite teas are
served by knowledgeable staff, that are
committed to ensuring their guests
are satisfied.

Overview

Year Opened
1865
Owner
Sheraton Hotels & Resorts
Restaurant Name
The Palm Court
Pastry Chef
Sarah Hartnett

Suppliers

Tea Supplier
Twinings
Coffee Supplier
Tchibo

RATING

CAKE
4.25 / 5

OVERALL
4.00 / 5
★ ★ ★ ★

The Ritz

150 Piccadilly, W1J 9BR

Afternoon Tea

Image supplied by The Ritz

Daily, seatings at 11:30am, 1:30pm, 3:30pm, 5:30pm and 7:30pm

Afternoon Tea

Traditional Afternoon Tea

Selection of sandwiches, freshly baked raisin and plain scones with clotted cream and strawberry preserve, tea cakes and pastries, with a selection of teas.

£42.00

Champagne Afternoon Tea

Traditional Afternoon Tea with a glass of Champagne.

£54.00

Celebration Tea

Traditional Afternoon Tea with a special cake.

£53.00

Celebration Tea with Champagne

Traditional Afternoon Tea with a glass of Champagne and a special cake.

£64.00

*T*he Ritz is world-renowned for delivering an exceptional afternoon tea experience – and that reputation is well deserved. Grand, luxurious and steeped in history, the menu is traditional and executed to a high standard. Cakes are truly beautiful, with mini delights including the decadent four chocolate Ritz cake, a dream come true for chocoholics. An endless supply of sandwiches, warm scones and pastries are served, while afternoon tea lovers relax within the institution's tasteful decor. Live piano is played in the background – the man responsible is often Frank Sinatra's former personal pianist and The Ritz house musician, Ian Gomez. Booking in advance for afternoon tea is strongly recommended, particularly on weekends. The most expensive on the pricing spectrum, The Ritz is not for those on a budget, but is sure to provide afternoon tea lovers with a quintessential British dining experience.

Contact

020 7493 8181
www.theritzlondon.com
tea@theritzlondon.com

Overview

Year Opened
1906
Owner
Sir David Barclay & Sir Frederick Barclay
Restaurant Name
Palm Court
Pastry Chef
Regis Beauregard

RATING

CAKE
4.25 / 5

OVERALL
4.75 / 5

The Sanderson

50 Berners Street, W1T 3NG

Image supplied by The Sanderson

 Open ....

Daily, seatings every half hour:
Mon-Fri. 2:00pm - 5:30pm,
Sat-Sun. 12:30pm - 5:30pm

Overview

Year Opened
2007
Owner
Morgans Hotel Group
Restaurant Name
Suka
Pastry Chef
David Dosso

Suppliers

Tea Supplier
Various
Coffee Supplier
L'Unico

Afternoon Tea

Mad Hatter's Afternoon Tea

Rainbow-coloured finger sandwiches, traditional scones and a variety of Alice in Wonderland-inspired desserts including Queen of Hearts Strawberries and Cream Mousse, and the Chocolate Opera Rabbit's Clock sponge cake.

£35.00

Contact

020 7300 5588
www.sandersonlondon.com

*T*he Sanderson invites afternoon tea lovers to tumble down the rabbit hole for a whimsical dining experience. Guests can sit in the modern Suka restaurant or plant-filled outdoor sanctuary and choose from a range of afternoon tea options. For those desiring a gastronomic adventure, The Mad Hatter's Afternoon Tea offers a weird and wonderful take on the British tradition. Among the quirky and unusual are rainbow-coloured finger sandwiches on saffron, spinach and beetroot bread, and a blueberry lollipop promising to turn tongues hot and cold. Labelled 'Drink Me', a bottled dessert containing layers of passion fruit jelly, a coconut panna cotta and exotic foam accompanies, delivering a different taste with each sip. Flowering teas are served in glass goblets. Delights are beautifully displayed on tea stands made from vintage tea sets, the perfect finishing touch for this celebration of the senses.

RATING

CAKE
4.50 / 5

OVERALL
4.50 / 5 ★★★★⯪

The Savoy

Strand, WC2R 0EU

Evoking an atmosphere of old-fashioned glamour, The Savoy's afternoon tea is held in the striking and recently refurbished Thames Foyer. Finger sandwiches, scones, delicious pastries and signature cakes are among the treats on offer. The stylish setting features an elegant glass cupola, allowing guests to enjoy afternoon tea amid the magnificent winter garden gazebo and shining natural light. The grand piano tinkles in the background, further adding to the tranquil ambiance. Inspired by champagne, cocktails and cabaret, the venue boasts dramatic jet-black and burnished gold hues. Take-home chocolates, pâtisserie, jams, tea and china can be purchased in The Savoy tea shop - here guests can also see pastry chefs and chocolatiers put the finishing touches on cakes and confectionery. The latest addition to the menu is the Art Decadent Tea, now served in the Beaufort Bar.

Overview

Year Opened
1889
Owner
Fairmont Hotels & Resorts
Restaurant Name
The Thames Foyer
Pastry Chef
Martin Chiffers

Suppliers

Tea Supplier
Jing Tea
Coffee Supplier
Rizzetti

Open

Daily, seatings twice an hour between 1:30pm and 5:45pm

Afternoon Tea

Traditional Afternoon Tea

A selection of finger sandwiches, freshly baked raisin and plain scones with cream, homemade lemon curd and strawberry preserve, French pastries, Thames Foyer signature cakes, a selection of teas.

£40.00

Traditional High Tea

A selection of finger sandwiches, toasted crumpets, Thames Foyer signature cakes, a selection of teas.

£42.50

Traditional Afternoon Tea with Champagne

The Traditional Afternoon Tea with a glass of Louis Roederer Brut NV or Ruinart Rose NV.

£51.50 / £54.00

Traditional High Tea with Champagne

The Traditional High Tea with a glass of Louis Roederer Brut NV or Ruinart Rose NV.

£54.00 / £56.50

Contact

020 7420 2111
www.fairmont.com
savoy@fairmont.com

RATING

CAKE
4.25 / 5

OVERALL
4.50 / 5

Image supplied by The Savoy

Afternoon Tea

Sketch

9 Conduit Street, W1S 2XG

*S*ketch is a fantastical, maximalist and opulent sensory delight. Renowned for its creative food, drink and entertainment styles, the eclectic establishment celebrates all things gastronomy and design related. The interior is nothing short of stunning and features include ostrich-egg-toilet-pods, crystal studded powder rooms, decadent lighting and a giant illuminated angel resembling an oversized jelly mould. Comfort food, divine signature sweets and decadent afternoon teas are available in the Parlour. Bookings are unnecessary. Here, the vibe is mellow, while still retaining an air of prestige. Signature sweet the Q & C gateau does not disappoint. Served on floral fine china with delicate silver cutlery, the chestnut mousse is ornamented with confit chestnut, poached quince, blueberry compote, macaronade biscuit and macadamia. The perfect balance is hit – it is beautifully creamy but not too sweet. Extensive teas and a selection of exotic coffees are also available. Afternoon tea includes a selection of sandwiches, scones and pastries. Other options include champagne afternoon tea and cream tea.

Overview

Year Opened
2002
Owner
Mourad Mazouz
Restaurant Name
The Parlour
Pastry Chef
Pierre Gagnaire & team

Suppliers

Tea Supplier
Jing Tea
Coffee Supplier
Nespresso

Contact

020 7659 4500
www.sketch.uk.com
info@sketch.uk.com

Open

Daily, seatings any time between 3:00pm and 6:00pm

Afternoon Tea

Sketch Afternoon Tea

Assorted finger sandwiches, fruit scones, Sketch pastries and a choice of teas.

£27.00

Sketch Afternoon Tea for Two

A lighter option comprised of assorted finger sandwiches, fruit scones, Sketch pastries and a choice of teas.

£52.00

Champagne Afternoon Tea

The Sketch Afternoon Tea served with a glass of Pommery Brut Royal, Pommery Springtime Rosé or Dom Pérignon.

£38.00 / £46.00 / £65.00

Cream Tea

Fruit scones with jam and clotted cream and a choice of teas.

£10.50

RATING

CAKE
4.50 / 5

OVERALL
4.75 / 5

Volupté

7-9 Norwich Street, EC4A 1EJ

Image supplied by Volupté

Afternoon Tea is served on the 1st & 3rd Saturday and the 2nd & 4th Sunday of the month at 2:30pm.

*S*erved with a side of a bewitching burlesque, Volupté offers afternoon tea with an unconventional twist. Treats are served in the cabaret salon, where guests can also enjoy live music, vaudeville comedy and circus performances. The somewhat decadent interior is a dimly lit space, reminiscent of a burlesque show set. Frilly curtains, a grand piano and corset-inspired lamps add to the sultry ambiance. The menu features sandwiches, scones, pastries and champagne - but the main attraction remains the burlesque extravaganzas. Ideal for a hen night or for those who crave something different, this afternoon tea experience is sure to be unforgettable.

Afternoon Tea

Afternoon Tease

A burlesque show accompanied by a selection of finger sandwiches, warm scones, homemade pastries, a selection of teas and a glass of champagne upon arrival.

£42.00

Contact

020 7831 1622
www.timefortease.co.uk
reservations@volupte-lounge.com

Overview

Year Opened
2006
Owner
Denise Farrell

Suppliers

Tea Supplier
Turners
Coffee Supplier
Turners

CAKE
3.00 / 5

OVERALL
4.00 / 5

RATING

The Waldorf Hilton Hotel

Aldwych, WC2B 4DD

Image supplied by The Waldorf Hilton

Open

Daily, seatings any time between
1:30pm and 4:30pm

*T*he iconic Waldorf Hilton offers a unique afternoon tea package that includes a historical tour of the hotel. Beautifully executed sandwiches, pastries, cakes and scones are on the menu. Many blends of tea are also available. Held in the Homage Patisserie - formerly the hotel's smoking room - the interior is lined with rich wood panelling and velvet seats. The soft piano from the foyer adds to the classical ambiance. The hotel also hosts tea dances in the beautiful Palm Court, a backdrop so grand it inspired the ballroom set in the movie Titanic.

Overview

Year Opened
1908
Owner
Hilton Hotels
Restaurant Name
Good Godfrey's Bar and Lounge

Suppliers

Tea Supplier
Twinings
Coffee Supplier
Illy

Afternoon Tea

Sparkling Afternoon Tea

Prosecco Fantinel Rosé, assortment of finger sandwiches, homemade scones with Devonshire clotted cream and preserve, homemade delicate pastries and selection of hot beverages.

£29.50

Champagne Afternoon Tea

Piper-Heidsieck Brut, assortment of finger sandwiches, homemade scones with Devonshire clotted cream and preserve, homemade delicate pastries and selection of hot beverages.

£34.50

Contemporary Afternoon Tea

Assortment of finger sandwiches, homemade scones with Devonshire clotted cream and preserve, homemade delicate pastry and selection of hot beverages.

£23.50

Contact

020 7836 2400
www.waldorfhilton.co.uk
pierre.antoine.lhommet@hilton.com

RATING

CAKE
4.25 / 5

OVERALL
4.25 / 5

The Wolseley

160 Piccadilly, W1J 9EB

*D*espite its relative youth, this luxury restaurant has emerged as one of London's most reputable fine eateries. Uniquely modern yet colonial in feel, the opulent interior showcases chandeliers and a wooden finish. The venue is constantly buzzing - a sure sign of a special place. The selections of tea - although limited - are lovely. The Wolseley afternoon blend is a beautifully robust flavour, and an ideal accompaniment to the selection of sandwiches, scones and pastries available. The fruit scones are an ideal consistency - light with a slight crumble. The brilliant Battenburg achieves just the right blend of sugar and almonds. But the real treat is the tier of beautiful pastries which are evidence of pastry chef Regis Negrier's incredible care and precision. Seasonal selections are perfectly balanced, no flavour, shape or colour dominates - delicate green pistachio macarons are complemented with rich, creamy cheesecake. Displayed on a silver stand with a silver tea pot, this elegant touch is sure to excite those looking for the ultimate English experience.

Overview

Year Opened
2003
Owner
Chris Corbin & Jeremy King
Pastry Chef
Regis Negrier

Suppliers

Tea Supplier
L'Unico
Coffee Supplier
L'Unico

Open

Daily, seatings any time between:
Mon-Fri.   3:00pm – 6:30pm
Sat-Sun.   3:30pm – 5:30pm

Afternoon Tea

Afternoon Tea

A classic option with finger sandwiches, fruit scones, pastries and a choice of teas.

£21.00

Champagne Tea

The Afternoon Tea with a glass of Pommery Brut Royal.

£29.75

Cream Tea

A lighter option of fruit scones with homemade jam and clotted cream.

£9.75

Contact

020 7499 6996
www.thewolseley.com
reservations@thewolseley.com

Find The Wolseley's Apple Poppy Seed Cake recipe on page 147

RATING

CAKE
4.00 / 5

OVERALL
4.50 / 5

Wedding Cakes

The History Of Wedding Cakes

The Development of the Wedding Cake

Almost all cultures celebrate special occasions with sweets and weddings are perhaps the best example of this custom. Wedding cakes have a long history, but the elegant traditional tiered wedding cakes we delight in today are far removed from their earliest origins.

A Roman Food Fight

Cakes were an important part of weddings as far back as 2,000 years ago, when Roman wedding cakes more closely resembled loaves of bread. Tradition dictated that the groom break the cake - a symbol of fertility - over his wife's head to signify his dominance and bring good luck to the couple.

Inventing the layer cake

Medieval wedding cakes were created from small buns brought by each guest as a gift. These buns would be stacked in a pile and sometimes frosted together with sugar. The bride and groom then attempted to kiss over the bun tower and success in doing so signified prosperity for the newlyweds.

Legend has it that the modern croquembouche (a cone-shaped stack of choux pastry balls filled with cream) was invented after a French pâtissier visited medieval England and recreated the traditional tower of cakes with sweet pastry. Famous French pastry chefs Avice and Carême later adapted the recipe using choux pastry to create what we now know as the croquembouche, and today it remains a popular wedding cake alternative throughout Europe.

In England, however, another visiting French chef changed the tradition dramatically during the 17th century by coming up with the idea of a solid stacked cake that avoided the inconvenience of piling the cakes into a mound. This innovation soon developed into the layer cake, a design that quickly caught on with couples.

The Modern Wedding Cake and its Traditions

Prepared days in advance, early wedding cakes were covered in lard to ensure they remained moist. Initially the lard was removed before being served, but later it was mixed with sugar and left on top of the cake as a form of icing.

In the Victorian era, white cakes symbolised the purity of the bride, but prior to this, wedding cakes were also coloured white to signify wealth, as perfectly white icing was only achieved by using the finest, most expensive, refined sugar.

Although the cutting of the cake now represents the first joint act of newlyweds, previously the bride cut the cake and handed slices to the groom's family. This act represented the transfer of her duties from her father's household to her husband's. This tradition ended when the development of multi-tiered cakes led to more solid icing that required the strength of both the bride and the groom to cut through it.

The development of multi-tiered wedding cakes is attributed to Thomas Rich, a baker's apprentice during the 18th century who fell in love with his boss's daughter. On their wedding day, Rich surprised his bride with a wedding cake inspired by the tiered steeple of St. Bride's Church in London. This cake marked the invention of the tiered wedding cake, and Rich made his fortune selling edible creations modelled on the church for the rest of his life.

Bompas & Parr

143 Wardour Street, W1F 8WA

*P*erfect for the bride and groom wishing to take a walk on the wild side, Bompas & Parr is famous for staging extraordinary jelly events. The creations of culinary enchanters Sam Bompas and Harry Parr have been exhibited worldwide, including in the San Francisco Museum of Modern Art and at the London Festival of Architecture. Often referred to as modern-day magicians, Bompas and Parr's concepts are produced in collaboration with cooks, technicians, architects and graphic designers. These innovators created a spectacular six-foot tall marshmallow tiered cake to celebrate the royal wedding of Prince William and Kate Middleton. They have also invented other leading-edge wonders, including a Willy Wonka-style flavour-changing chewing gum.

Open

By appointment only

Overview

Year Opened
2007
Owner
Sam Bompas & Harry Parr

Price Range

Price on application. Customised wedding jellies from £800.

Contact

020 7403 9403
www.jellymongers.co.uk
info@jellymongers.co.uk

The Cake Parlour

146 Arthur Road, SW19 8AQ

*T*he Cake Parlour's founder Zoe Clark specialises in extravagant and luxurious hand-sculpted wedding cakes specifically tailored to suit each individual couple. Crafted with great attention to detail, opulently decorated cakes can feature more traditional flowers, lace work and piping, or vivacious colours, patterns and sugar models. All cakes are made using the finest ingredients and are available in a range of flavours. Designs turn inspired ideas into mouth-watering works of art. Also on offer are bespoke Sweet Tables which can include macaron towers, bon bon jars, meringues, cake pops, petit fours, cupcake fancies and lollipops.

Open

By appointment only

Overview

Year Opened
2010
Owner & Cake Designer
Zoe Clark

Price Range

Price confirmed upon consultation. Three-tier wedding cakes from £450.

Contact

020 8947 4424
www.thecakeparlour.com
info@thecakeparlour.com

Elizabeth's Cake Emporium

Station Road, EN5 1QP

Image supplied by Elizabeth's

Open

By appointment only

Overview

Year Opened
2006
Owner & Cake Designer
Elizabeth Solaru

Price Range

Price on application. Wedding cakes from £250.

Contact

079 5806 9116
www.elizabethscakeemporium.com
info@elizabethscakeemporium.com

Cake designer Elizabeth Solaru creates amazing cakes that will dazzle the eye and the taste buds of any bride and groom. Elizabeth's Cake Emporium has a prestigious list of clients including celebrities, royalty, TV shows, five-star hotels and glamorous West End stores. Renowned for her intricate designs, Solaru's cakes are adorned with amazing bridal-inspired sugar-cast flower displays, peacock feathers and jewellery. Structures include tiered, traditional and towers of treats, and flavours such as triple chocolate delight, Elizabeth's secret recipe fruit cake and the Bailey's Irish Cream cake are best-sellers. Elizabeth's Cake Emporium also creates specialty children's cakes, cookies, cupcakes and birthday cakes. Designs have attracted a great deal of media attention, with wedding cakes featured in glamorous national and international publications.

Janet Mohapi-Banks

85 Hook Road, KT19 8TP

Award-winning cake designer Janet Mohapi-Banks treats her sculptural wedding cake designs much like detailed artworks. Cakes are tailored to each individual marriage ceremony and consultations are carried out to ensure the cake is everything desired. The signature wedding cake, Rose, features 300 hand-crafted sugar roses, and the Forget-Me-Not cake is topped with 1,600 hand-cut and piped flowers. Perfect for fashionistas, Mohapi-Banks' acclaimed Jimmy Choo design features three rich chocolate brownie cakes, iced in pink sugar paste, with a hand-painted Jimmy Choo logo. All cakes are handmade and designed using high-quality ingredients. A variety of bespoke cake flavours are available including rich chocolate and orange zest sponge.

Open

By appointment only

Overview

Year Opened
2009
Owner & Cake Designer
Janet Mohapi-Banks

Price Range

Price on application. Tiered cakes from £1200.

Contact

077 2557 8450
www.janetmohapibanks.com
cakes@janetmohapibanks.com

Little Venice Cake Company

15 Manchester Mews, W1U 2DX

Mich Turner MBE has designed couture cakes for celebrities and royalty including Her Majesty the Queen, Madonna, Gordon Ramsay and David Beckham. Her creations reflect the breathtaking and cutting-edge designs that have positioned her among London's best wedding cake designers. Using only the finest ingredients, the Little Venice Cake Company provides three ranges of wedding cakes: the Crown range, featuring the John Galliano-inspired glitter rainbow roses - a kaleidoscopic creation topped with glitter-encrusted roses; the Iced range, including the couture rock and rose cake encased in 24-carat gold and embellished with gold leaves and noir roses; and the Chocolate range, featuring an array of milk, white and dark chocolate creations. Master classes taught by Turner herself are also available.

Open

By appointment only

Overview

Year Opened
1999
Owner & Cake Designer
Mich Turner MBE

Price Range

Price on application. Wedding cakes from £300.

Contact

020 7486 5252
www.lvcc.co.uk
info@lvcc.co.uk

Maisie Fantaisie

8 Cherry Laurel Walk, SW2 2DA

Renowned for its beautifully designed and detailed cakes, this highly reputable wedding cake establishment comes recommended by top wedding venues, and is regularly featured in glossy wedding publications. Founder May Clee-Cadman creates opulent bespoke celebration cakes fit for a fairytale. With a background in art and design and a passion for baking and sugarcraft, Clee-Cadman has emerged as one of London's leading cake makers. Using only the best ingredients, Clee-Cadman ensures her cakes taste as delightful as they look. Moist, delicious and available in a range of flavours, Maisie Fantaisie's clients can select their own combination of cakes, buttercreams and preserves. Among the favourites is the coconut cake with coconut buttercream and raspberry preserve. Wedding cake consultations and tastings are also available.

Open

By appointment only

Overview

Year Opened
2003
Owner & Cake Designer
May Clee-Cadman

Price Range

Price on application. Wedding cakes from £315.

Contact

020 8671 5858
www.maisiefantaisie.co.uk
enquiries@maisiefantaisie.co.uk

Maki's Cakes

17 Riversdell Close, Chertsey, Surrey, KT16 9J3

Founded by Makiko "Maki" Searle, Maki's Cakes creates an immaculate collection of ornate tiered, individual and signature wedding cakes. Maki studied food art in Tokyo, where she went on to become a French pastry chef. Among her specialities is the Temari individual cake, which is inspired by the ancient Japanese art of weaving colourful silk to create a ball. Maki's elegant cakes can be styled to suit any wedding by incorporating themed colours or designs inspired by wedding dress details. Maki's many elaborate creations include the festive colourful poppy cake and the retro cake.

Open

By appointment only

Overview

Year Opened
2007
Owner & Cake Designer
Makiko Searle

Price Range

Price on application. Wedding cakes are £600 on average.

Contact

019 3256 2403
www.makiscakes.com
maki@makiscakes.com

Peggy Porschen Weddings

116 Ebury Street, SW1W 9QQ

Images supplied by Peggy Porschen

*F*ounded by award-winning cake designer Peggy Porschen, this Belgravia-based cake parlour offers exquisite wedding cakes handcrafted by master bakers, patissiers and sugar artists. Choose from an abundance of bespoke tiered cakes, mini cakes and cookies. Each creation is a work of art - to look at and to taste, and among the most romantic is the luxurious couture lace tiered cake. Inspired by an Oscar de la Renta wedding dress, this showpiece is decorated with intricately hand-crafted sugar lace embroidery and finished with a cluster of sugar roses and stephanotis. The popular bride and groom cookies provide a fun option and can be customised to replicate actual wedding outfits. Set within a bubble-gum pink coloured Georgian-style building, the surroundings of Peggy Porschen Weddings are just as special as the cakes within.

Open

Mon-Sat.	9:00am - 6:00pm
Sun.	10:00am - 6:00pm

or by appointment

Overview

Year Opened
2003
Owner & Cake Designer
Peggy Porschen & Bryn Morrow

Price Range

Price on application. Wedding cakes from £500.

Contact

020 7730 1716
www.peggyporschen.com
info@peggyporschen.com

Rachelle's

29 Christian Fields, SW16 3JY

Cake designer Rachel Hill has a background as an art director and loves to create both original, innovative designs for contemporary brides, and stunning, elegant cakes for more traditional clients. Her exceptional service and real flair for design have led to acclaim from customers and the industry, landing her a place in the finals for last year's Celebration Cake Maker of the Year in the Baking Industry Awards.

Open

By appointment only

Overview

Year Opened
2007
Owner & Cake Designer
Rachel Hill

Price Range

Wedding cakes start at £225 for a single tier.

Contact

079 5871 4672
www.rachelles.co.uk
cakes@rachelles.co.uk

Rosalind Miller Cakes

11 Ewart Road, Forest Hill, SE23 1AY

Rosalind Miller's unique and edible wedding masterpieces are home-baked using specially created recipes and organic ingredients wherever possible. Producing exquisite designs with a contemporary romantic feel, Miller's background in fine arts and textile design shines through in her creations – she has even pioneered a technique of cutting intricate designs from icing to overlay onto cakes. The Marie Antoinette cupcakes and ivory rose tiered cake are among the stunning wedding cakes available. Miller's stylish wedding cake creations have also been featured in Vogue. Originally taught to bake by her mother, Miller is also the brains behind the inspiring Peggy's Cupcakes.

Open

By appointment only

Overview

Year Opened
2010
Owner & Cake Designer
Rosalind Miller

Price Range

Price on application. Wedding cakes from £350.

Contact

079 5757 1797
www.rosalindmillercakes.com
info@rosalindmillercakes.com

Chocolate
& Sweets

Charbonnel et Walker Old Bond Street

One The Royal Arcade, 28 Old Bond Street, W1S 4BT

*O*ne of Britain's earliest chocolatiers, Charbonnel et Walker is the story of a partnership initially supported by the then Prince of Wales, Edward VII. Today this institution is endorsed by the Royal Warrant as chocolate manufacturers to Her Majesty the Queen. The store design and packaging exudes an olde worlde elegance. The collection of chocolates is extensive and includes world-renowned speciality English Rose and Violet Creams, and best-selling Pink Marc de Champagne Truffles. Charbonnel et Walker is also known for its luscious dark chocolate, made from fine dark Couverture.

Sister Locations

Canary Wharf, Liverpool Street Station, Harrods and Selfridges

Open

Mon-Sat.	10:00am - 6:00pm
Sun.	Closed

Overview

Year Opened
1875

Contact

020 7318 2075
www.charbonnel.co.uk
enquiries@charbonnel.co.uk

Fortnum & Mason Food Hall

181 Piccadilly, W1A 1ER

*T*his fine British institution has been selling high-quality sweet treats to fine food lovers for hundreds of years. Set in a plush multi-level department store, the food hall is located in the very heart of London's Piccadilly.
The Georgian-style interior features an opulent chandelier, regal red carpet and a luxurious central chocolate counter overflowing with pastel-coloured delights. On the ground floor is a beautiful array of confectionery, biscuits, cakes, pastries and freshly baked goods from the Fortnum and Mason in-store bakery. Visitors from around the world are spoilt for choice with a wide range of gift boxes, a library of chocolate bars and beautiful handmade truffles.

Open

Mon-Sat.	10:00am - 8:00pm
Sun.	12:00pm - 6:00pm

Overview

Year Opened
1707

Contact

0845 300 1707
www.fortnumandmason.com

Green Valley

36-37 Upper Berkeley Street, W1H 5QF

Bringing a touch of the Middle East to West London, Green Valley is an Arabic-inspired supermarket offering irresistible displays of sweet treats. Under the vintage green-and-white striped awning, the front window is filled with tempting delights. The extensive patisserie selection includes an array of cakes, as well as Green Valley's delicious exotic signature pastry, baklava. Packaged products are stacked high on shelves, while a range of traditional homemade goods are proudly placed on silver cake stands. High-quality fresh produce and Middle Eastern savoury delights are also available.

Open

Daily:	8:00am - 12:00pm

Overview

Year Opened
1986

Contact

020 7402 7385
www.green-valley.co
info@green-valley.co

Hope & Greenwood Covent Garden

1 Russell Street, WC2B 5JD

Exuding a nostalgic ambiance and offering a vast assortment of colourful candy, Hope & Greenwood transports candy-lovers to a 1950s sweet-treat heaven. Stocking an array of British classics, the collection spans favourites including sherbet pips, flying saucers, and lemon bon-bons. As well as a core mix of sweets and chocolate, the shop also offers seasonal specials. Sweets are encased in old-fashioned jars, boxes and tins and are tightly packed in floor-to-ceiling shelves. The atmosphere is quaint, with an olde worlde British feel. The unique branding and recipes are created by founders Miss Hope and Mr Greenwood. A delightful experience, complete with good old-fashioned customer service.

Sister Locations

Dulwich and Selfridges

Open

Mon-Fri.	11:00am - 7:30pm
Sat.	10:30am - 7:30pm
Sun.	12:00pm - 6:00pm

Overview

Year Opened
2004
Owner
Miss Hope & Mr Greenwood

Contact

020 7240 3314
www.hopeandgreenwood.co.uk
missdollymixture@hopeandgreenwood.co.uk

138

La Maison du Chocolat

41-46 Piccadilly, W1J 0DS

Image supplied by La Maison du Chocolat

Perfect for those in the mood to indulge, this high-end chocolatier specialises in classic and seasonal chocolates. Chocolate connoisseurs can sit back in the Piccadilly store's luxurious surroundings and enjoy the acclaimed pastry collection, as well as a hot chocolate from the small coffee shop within. Themes of wood and marble run throughout the store, and staff happily assist customers to select sweet treats to enjoy in store or take home. The chocolate collection features delectable ganaches, pralines and fruited chocolates. Other sweet wonders include scrumptious macarons, tarts and éclairs.

Sister Locations

Harrods and Selfridges

Open

Mon-Sat.	10:00am - 7:00pm
Sun.	12:00pm - 6:00pm

Overview

Year Opened
2004
Owner
Robert Linxe

Contact

020 7287 8500
www.lamaisonduchocolat.co.uk
customer@lamaisonduchocolat.co.uk

Melt Chocolates

59 Ledbury Road, W11 2AA

Set in the heart of Notting Hill, this chocolate boutique is a hub of creativity. Customers can experience world-class luxurious truffles being hand made in the kitchen. The wonderful ranges of recipes are designed in-house by chocolatiers. Those who love truffles can keep watch for exclusive collaborations with top chefs. Amid the plethora of fresh chocolates are the tantalising chilli cubes, ginger and passion fruit cups, and the peanut butter and raspberry jam bonbon. Lollipop lovers are treated to best-seller, entitled Beau by Celia Birtwell - a milk-chocolate lollipop featuring the British style icon's adorable dog design. Luxury chocolate bars and hot chocolate products are also available.

Sister Locations

Selfridges

Open

Mon-Sat.	10:00am - 6:30pm
Sun.	11:00am - 4:00pm

Overview

Year Opened
2006
Owner
Louise Nason

Contact

020 7727 5030
www.meltchocolates.com
ledbury@meltchocolates.com

Minamoto Kitchoan

44 Piccadilly, W1J 0DS

Minamoto Kitchoan offers a highly traditional Japanese cake and confectionery experience. The high-quality wagashi (a Japanese term for confectionery) is made using only natural ingredients - often entirely from plants. Treats are accompanied by a short description of the ingredients within. Once chosen, these are served with a complimentary green tea. Chocolate lovers can prepare to delight in the Chocolat Mochisyocramochi, comprised of pure chocolate wrapped in rice cake topped with cocoa powder. Traditionally Japanese in layout, the minimal white walls are complemented by clean-lined glass displays showcasing painstakingly prepared sweets. Japanese rock gardens, quirky mobiles and vivid kanji prints add an individual touch. As you would expect, take-home souvenirs come meticulously packaged.

Open

Mon-Fri.	10:00am - 7:00pm
Sat.	10:00am - 8:00pm
Sun.	Closed

Overview

Year Opened
1997
Owner
Takushi Okada

Contact

020 7437 3135
www.kitchoan.com
minamoto@kitchoan.f2s.com

Paul A Young Wardour Street

143 Wardour Street, W1F 8WA

Paul A Young's boutique chocolaterie draws on the unusual and blends the unexpected. Set in Soho's bustling Wardour Street, this new flagship store continues to perfect unthinkable culinary combinations – chocolate with Marmite, for example. The interior space features warm wooden tables and tones (the colour of chocolate) with mulberry trimmings, and exquisite displays of award-winning delicacies. Handmade onsite every day, the collection spans house truffles, artisan chocolate bars, ice cream and hot chocolate. The chocolate brownie and the signature sea-salted caramel truffle are among the array of blissful delights.

Sister Locations

Islington and Threadneedle Street

Open

Mon-Sat.	10:00am - 8:00pm
Sun.	12:00pm - 7:00pm

Overview

Year Opened
2011
Owner
Paul Young

Contact

020 7437 0011
www.paulayoung.co.uk

Prestat

14 Princes Arcade, SW1Y 6DS

his wonderful world of vibrant colours and swirls is so fantastical, Roald Dahl mentioned its truffles in his book 'My Uncle Oswald'. Prestat's divine chocolates have received two Royal Warrants, and the bright blue interior is decorated with a picture of Her Majesty the Queen. Shelves spill over with handcrafted chocolates marvellously packaged in bright boxes designed by renowned artist Kitty Arden. The perfect treat, Prestat believes the Choxi+ bars are so rich in antioxidants they should be part of any balanced diet! Located in a quaint arcade off Piccadilly, this delightful store is a lovely escape from the nearby hustle and bustle.

Open

Mon-Fri.	9:30am - 6:00pm
Sat.	10:00am - 5:00pm
Sun.	Closed

Overview

Year Opened
1902
Owner
Nick Crean & Bill Keeling

Contact

0800 021 3023
www.prestat.co.uk
customer@prestat.co.uk

Rabot Estate

2 Stoney Street, SE1 9AA

abot Estate is a cacao producer based on the Caribbean island of St. Lucia, and a chocolate shop and café nestled within the gastronomic hub that is Borough Market. Attracting foodies and chocolate lovers alike, the unique chocolate café boasts an innovative menu that is based on a variety of sweet and savoury cocoa-based wraps. A variety of chocolate drinks are also offered, including the award-winning drinking chocolate and cocoa tea. This is the latest chocolatier to be opened by Hotel Chocolat founders Angus Thirlwell and Peter Harris. Rustic in feel, the interior features reclaimed materials to replicate the weathered ambiance of a St. Lucian rum shack.

Open

Mon-Wed.	8:00am - 6:00pm
Thur.	7:30am - 6:00pm
Fri.	7:30am - 6:30pm
Sat.	9:00am - 6:30pm
Sun.	Closed

Overview

Owner
Angus Thirlwell & Peter Harris
Pastry Chef
Oliver Nicod

Contact

020 7403 9852
www.rabotestate.com
borough@rabotestate.com

Rococo Chocolates Belgravia

5 Motcomb Street, SW1X 8JU

Find Rococo Chocolates'
Orange and Almond Cake
by Claudia Roden
on page 152

One of London's best hand-crafted chocolate stores, Rococo Chocolates was developed by its founder Chantal Coady to push the boundaries of chocolate retailing. In a revolt against mass-market sweets, the cartel started with a campaign for real chocolate. At the Belgravia flagship store, chocolate fanatics can enjoy a creamy hot chocolate in the MaRococo secret garden, or stay inside and observe chocolatiers work their magic concocting new truffles. Over 50 flavours of pristinely packaged chocolate bars are on display, including the Lavender Organic Dark Chocolate and the Basil and Persian Lime Chocolate. Rococo also sells extra special hand-painted chocolate art. Displaying incredible craftsmanship, Rococo's creations are so spectacular that they were featured in the film 'Chocolat'.

Open

Mon-Sat.	10:00am - 6:30pm
Sun.	12:00pm - 6:00pm

Overview

Year Opened
2007
Owner
James Booth & Chantal Coady

Contact

020 7245 0993
www.rococochocolates.com
5motcombstreet@rococochocolates.com

Sister Locations

Chelsea, Marylebone and King's Road

William Curley Belgravia

198 Ebury Street, SW1W 8UN

TOP
20

Widely regarded as a chocolate and patisserie genius, William Curley has won the Academy of Chocolate's Best British Chocolatier award for five consecutive years. In 2009, he joined forces with fellow chocolatier and wife, Suzue Curley, to create a chocolate heaven within their Belgravia boutique. The collection offers an exquisite selection of traditionally flavoured truffles, a Nostalgia Range of chocolate classics and diversity of hot drinking chocolates and chocolate nibbles. A special dessert bar menu and a wide selection of ice cream are also available.

Sister Locations

Richmond-Upon-Thames and Harrods

Open

Mon-Thur.	9:00am - 7:00pm
Fri-Sat.	9:30am - 8:00pm
Sun.	9:30am - 6:30pm

Dessert Bar open Saturday 1:00pm - 8:00pm and Sunday 1:00pm - 6:00pm

Overview

Year Opened
2009
Owner
William Curley

Contact

020 7730 5522
www.williamcurley.co.uk

Chocolate & Sweets

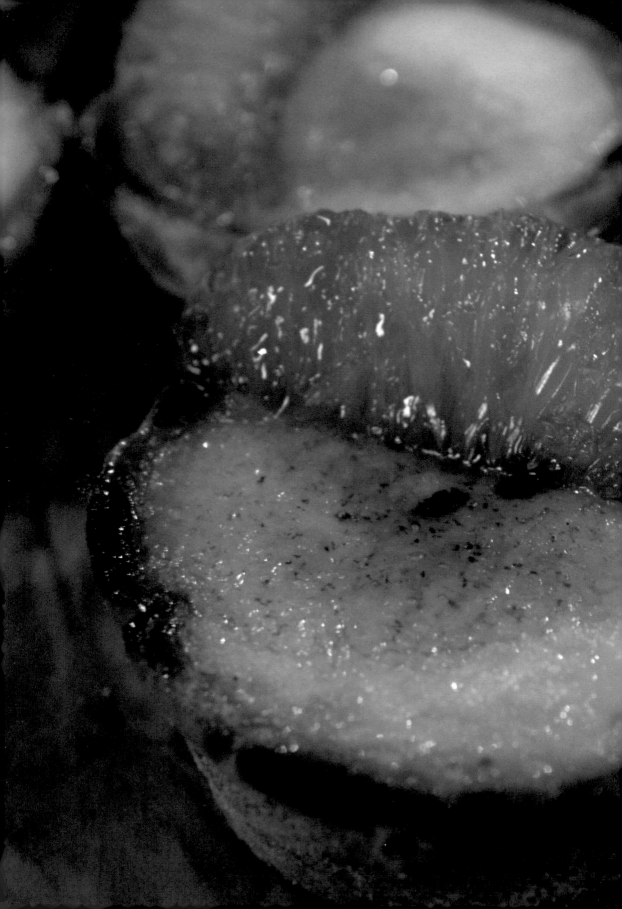

The
Recipes

Apple Poppy Seed Cake by The Wolseley

Makes 6 servings

Cooking time
45-50 minutes

Equipment
2 rectangular cake tins, 26cm x 9cm
Baking paper

Ingredients
250g butter
250g icing sugar
5g lemon zest
Pinch of salt
6 egg yolks
4 apples, grated and strained (400g)
6 egg whites
100g caster sugar
220g ground almonds
140g poppy seeds
60g rice flour

Method

1. Preheat the oven to 170°C (340°F). Grease and line the cake tins.

2. Beat together the butter, icing sugar, lemon zest and salt until light and pale. Gradually add the egg yolks, beating well after each addition.

3. Peel and grate the apples.

4. In a separate bowl, combine the ground almonds, poppy seeds and rice flour.

5. Whip the egg whites and caster sugar together until the mixture forms soft peaks.

6. Mix a quarter of the apples, a quarter of the dry ingredients and a quarter of the egg whites into the butter mixture. Repeat this process until all ingredients have been incorporated.

7. Pour 1000g of the mixture into each tin and bake for approximately 45-50 minutes.

Presentation
Trim the ends of the cake and cut into six equal pieces. Hold a palette knife over the centre of the cakes and dust the edges with neige decor.

Bakewell Tarts & Vanilla Buttercream
By Lily Vanilli

Cooking time
25-30 minutes

Equipment
1 sieve
1 heavy-bottomed pan
1 piping bag
1 cupcake pan

Bakewell Tarts

Ingredients

For the pastry:

250g quality plain flour (we recommend W&H Marriage & Sons), plus extra for dusting
50g icing sugar
125g cold butter, cut into small cubes
1 large free-range egg, beaten
Zest of 1 orange
A splash of milk

For the coulis:

200g bag frozen mixed berries
50g caster sugar
50ml water

For the frangipane:

85g unsalted butter at room temperature
85g golden caster sugar
85g ground almonds
Finely grated zest of 1 orange
1 egg

Optional extras: toasted flaked almonds, fresh cherries

Method

Pastry:

1. Preheat the oven to 190°C (375°F).

2. From a height, sieve the flour, then the sugar, onto a clean surface.

3. Work in the butter using your thumbs and fingers to achieve a fine, crumbly mixture.

4. Add the egg, orange zest and milk and gently work mixture into a ball of dough. Flour lightly.

5. Pat into a flat round, wrap in cling-film and refrigerate for a minimum of half an hour.

Coulis:

1. While the pastry is cooling, place all of the coulis ingredients into a heavy-bottomed pan.

2. Heat gently and bring to the boil, stirring continuously.

3. Reduce to a simmer and heat until thickened. Allow to cool.

Frangipane:

Make the frangipane by beating all ingredients together until smooth. Spoon into a piping bag.

Vanilla Buttercream

Ingredients

55g unsalted butter at room temperature
250g icing sugar
4 tbsp almond meal
Approximately 1/2 cup double cream to taste

Method

1. Beat the butter for 5 minutes.

2. Add the sugar, almond meal and 1/4 cup cream, beating slowly. Continue to gradually add cream until desired thickness is reached and the mixture is smooth and light. This usually takes approximately 3 minutes.

Assembly

1. Roll out the pastry, cut into rounds to fit a cupcake pan and press them into place.

2. Spoon in some of the coulis, pipe in the frangipane and top with flaked almonds.

3. Bake the tarts for 25-30 minutes or until golden brown.

4. Cool, top with a dab of buttercream and top with a fresh cherry and toasted flaked almonds.

Banana Bread by Kaffeine

Cooking time

45 minutes

Equipment

1 food processor

1 baking loaf tin

Baking paper

Ingredients

200g sugar

100g butter

2 bananas, chopped

1 egg

1 tsp baking powder

½ tsp baking soda

1 tsp vanilla

300g plain flour

½ tsp cinnamon

1 tbsp honey

1 banana for garnish

Method

1. Preheat oven to 180°C (350°F).

2. In food processor, blend sugar and butter until pale and creamy.

3. Add two chopped bananas, egg, baking powder, baking soda and vanilla until well combined.

4. Sift flour and cinnamon into the mixture as it processes.

5. Line loaf tin with baking paper.

6. Evenly pour batter into the tin.

7. Bake for 45 minutes or until golden brown.

Presentation

Cut last banana in half lengthways and place on top of banana bread. Glaze entire loaf with honey.

Chocolate Bread & Butter Pudding
by Lanka

Preparation time

30 minutes

Cooking time

30-40 minutes

Equipment

1.5L shallow dish (ovenproof)

Ingredients

4-5 pain au chocolat (thinly sliced)

1 large egg yolk

3 large whole eggs

90g caster sugar

80g cocoa powder

80g dark chocolate, broken into small pieces

300ml double cream, heated until just boiling

100g roasted almonds

Method

1. Preheat the oven to 150°C (300°F).

2. Arrange the slices of pain au chocolat in overlapping layers in the dish.

3. Beat the egg yolk, whole eggs and sugar together in a large bowl.

4. Add cocoa powder and chocolate, and beat in the hot cream.

5. Slowly pour mixture over the bread.

6. Leave to stand for 20 minutes to allow the bread to soak up the chocolate custard.

7. Sprinkle with roasted almonds and bake for 30-40 minutes.

Chocolate Chip Whoopie Pie by Violet

Makes 9 large or 24 small Whoopie Pies

Cooking time
8-12 minutes

Equipment
2 baking trays
Roll of baking/parchment paper
Ice cream scoop
1 electric stand mixer

Chocolate Chip Whoopie Pie
Ingredients
280g plain flour
1 tsp baking powder
1½ tsp bicarbonate of soda
¼ tsp salt
125g unsalted butter, softened
100g sugar
100g light brown sugar
1 large egg
120ml buttermilk
1 tsp pure vanilla extract
200g dark chocolate chips

Method

1. Preheat oven to 180°C (350°F).

2. Line two trays with baking paper.

3. In a bowl, sift together the flour, baking powder and bicarbonate of soda. Stir in the salt. Set aside.

4. In the bowl of the mixer, using a flat beater, cream the softened butter and sugars until light and fluffy. Add the egg and mix well.

5. Measure the buttermilk into a jug, then add the vanilla. Pour the liquid into the butter mixture and beat until well combined.

6. Slowly add dry ingredients in two portions, mixing until just incorporated. Add the chocolate chips.

7. Chill for 30 minutes.

8. Use a 4cm ice cream scoop with a trigger (for large whoopies), or a mini scoop or melon-baller (for small whoopies), to place portions of batter about 5cm apart onto the prepared baking trays.

9. For large whoopies, bake for 10-12 minutes. For small whoopies, bake for 8-10 minutes. The cakes are ready when the touch of a finger leaves a slight depression in the surface.

10. Remove from oven and cool completely before filling.

Chocolate marshmallow filling
Ingredients
100g dark chocolate, broken into small pieces
3 egg whites
150g caster sugar
2 tbsp golden syrup
Pinch of salt
1 tsp pure vanilla extract

Method

1. Melt the chocolate in a heatproof bowl over a pan of barely simmering water.

2. Once the chocolate has melted, take the bowl off the pan and let it cool slightly while you prepare the marshmallow.

3. Place the saucepan of water back on the heat and bring to the boil. Weigh the remaining ingredients into the stainless steel bowl of a stand mixer, then place the bowl over the pot.

4. Whisk continuously by hand until the sugar has dissolved and the mixture is frothy and slightly opaque (about 10-15 minutes).

5. Remove bowl from heat and transfer contents to the mixer.

6. Whip the mixture on high speed until it is white, thick and holds its shape. Fold in the melted chocolate.

7. Pipe or spread the filling onto the flat surface of a cooled whoopie. Top it with another whoopie to make a sandwich and serve.

Claudia Rodens Orange & Almond Cake
by Rococo Chocolates

Cooking time
50-60 minutes

Equipment
1 x 24cm springform cake tin

Roll of baking paper

Ingredients
Butter for the tin

2 large oranges, washed (or 3 medium blood oranges)

250g caster sugar

6 eggs, separated

250g ground almonds

1 tsp baking powder

Icing sugar to dust

Method
1. Preheat the oven to 190°C (375°F).

2. Butter the cake tin and line the bottom with a round of baking paper.

3. Boil the whole, unpeeled oranges in a covered saucepan for about 1 1/2 hours, or until completely soft.

4. Discard the water. Once the oranges have cooled, cut them open and take out any pips and seeds.

5. Put the oranges in a food processor with the sugar, egg yolks, ground almonds and baking powder, and pulse until well combined.

6. Whisk the egg whites until soft peaks form.

7. Gently fold the orange mixture into the beaten egg whites in batches.

8. Pour the cake mix into the buttered cake tin and bake for 10 minutes before reducing the temperature to 160°C.

9. Continue to bake for about 50-60 minutes or until the cake pulls away from the sides of the tin.

10. Place cake on a wire rack to cool. Finish with a dusting of icing sugar.

Tip: To make an orange syrup to go with the cake, combine equal quantities of sugar and water and simmer with two chopped oranges for 15-20 minutes. This syrup is also great with yoghurt or crème fraiche for dessert.

The Recipes

Lemon Cupcakes by Love Bakery

Makes 12 cupcakes

Cooking time

25 minutes

Equipment

12-hole muffin tin

12 muffin cases

Zester or grater

Free-standing electric mixer

Mixing bowl

Spatula

Ice cream scoop, size 16

Wire rack

Medium piping bag and large star piping nozzle, or palette knife

Ingredients

For the cupcakes:

125g unsalted butter at room temperature

125g caster sugar

1 tbsp grated lemon zest

2 eggs at room temperature

125g self-raising flour

½ tsp baking powder

3 tbsp semi-skimmed milk

For the frosting:

125g unsalted butter, at room temperature

1 tsp grated lemon zest

½ tsp lemon extract

250g icing sugar, sifted

1 tbsp semi-skimmed milk

Yellow paste food colouring

Method

1. Preheat the oven to 180°C (350°F) and place muffin cases in the tins.

2. Add the butter, caster sugar and lemon zest into the electric mixer. Mix for 7 minutes until light and fluffy.

3. Add eggs one at a time and mix for 2 minutes.

4. In a separate bowl, combine flour and baking powder, then add to the mixture. Add milk and mix for a further minute.

5. When fully mixed, use an ice cream scoop to measure mixture into muffin cases.

6. Bake for 25 minutes. When cooked, leave to cool completely before icing.

7. To make the frosting, combine all ingredients but the colouring and mix well. Add colouring gradually until desired shade is reached. Spoon into a piping bag to ice cupcakes, or simply spread with a palette knife.

Optional extras

Sugar paste roses, leaves, daisies and butterflies.

Meringues by Bea's of Bloomsbury

Makes 40 mini meringues. For giant meringues, simply place larger amounts on the baking sheets.

Cooking time

50-60 minutes

Equipment

2 baking sheets

Electric whisk

Baking paper

Pastry brush

Ingredients

6 egg whites

350g (1 3/4 cups) caster/superfine sugar

150ml (2/3 cup) store-bought raspberry coulis for decoration

Method

1. Preheat oven to 110°C (215°F) or gas mark 1-2.

2. Fill a large saucepan 1/3 full of water. Heat over a medium low heat until simmering.

3. Lightly mix egg whites and sugar in a wide, shallow metal bowl.

4. Place the bowl over the pan of simmering water (making sure that the bottom of the bowl doesn't touch the water) and slowly heat the mixture until it is warm to the touch and the sugar has dissolved. Stir occasionally.

5. Remove from the heat and whisk with an electric whisk until stiff, glossy peaks are formed.

6. Dot a bit of mixture in each corner of the baking sheets and stick the baking paper to it.

7. Using two tablespoons, scoop golf ball-sized blobs of mixture onto the prepared baking sheets. Bake for 50-60 minutes until firm.

8. Remove meringues from the oven and, using a pastry brush, paint them with raspberry coulis. Return meringues to the oven and bake until the coulis has turned a darker, more purplish colour and the meringue is dry to the touch. The coulis can feel slightly sticky.

9. Remove from the oven and cool. Remove meringues from the baking paper and store in an airtight container for up to one week.

Orange & Lavender Cake by Cake Boy

Preparation time

30 minutes

Cooking time

1 hour

Equipment

1 x 20cm cake tin

Ingredients

400ml sunflower oil, plus extra for greasing

350g ground almonds

300g caster sugar

3 tsp baking powder

8 eggs

1 lemon

2 oranges, ideally Seville

2 tsp dried lavender

For the syrup:

Juice of the zested lemon and oranges above

100g caster sugar

A few cloves

2 tsp ground cinnamon

Method

1. Preheat the oven to 180°C (350°F) or gas mark 4. Grease a 20cm cake tin with extra oil, then line the base with baking paper.

2. In a mixing bowl, thoroughly combine the ground almonds, caster sugar and baking powder. Break in the eggs, add the oil and mix gently.

3. Using a fine grater, grate the zest from the lemon and oranges into the mixture. Add dried lavender and combine.

4. Turn the cake mixture into the prepared tin and bake for 1 hour. Cover the top with a piece of foil after about 20 minutes.

5. Meanwhile, make the syrup. Squeeze the juice from the zested lemon and oranges into a small pan. Add the sugar and spices, then mix well. Bring to the boil, then reduce the heat and simmer for 3 minutes.

6. Once the cake has been removed from the oven, pierce it several times with a skewer or small, sharp knife.

7. Using a tablespoon, spoon the syrup over the cake and allow it to soak in.

Tip: If you prefer a cake with a slightly less dense texture, substitute 50% of the ground almonds for finely ground polenta or semolina.

Rhubarb & Amaretto Cake
by The Haberdashery

Cooking time

50 minutes

Equipment

1 non-stick roasting tin

2 x 20cm sandwich tins

Baking paper

Sieve

Ingredients

400g rhubarb

200g caster sugar

225g softened unsalted butter, with more for greasing

150g amaretti biscuits

150g self-raising flour

4 medium eggs

½ tsp baking powder

150ml double cream

Icing sugar for dusting

Method

1. Preheat the oven to 200°C (390°F) or gas mark 6 (180°C for fan-assisted ovens).

2. Trim and cut the rhubarb into 3cm lengths and transfer to a non-stick roasting tin.

3. Sprinkle the rhubarb with 50g of the caster sugar and bake for 25 minutes or until the rhubarb softens and begins to caramelise. Remove it from the oven and allow to cool.

4. Reduce the oven temperature to 180°C or gas mark 4. Grease and line two 20cm sandwich tins with butter and baking paper.

5. Crush the biscuits in a bag using a rolling pin until finely ground.

6. Tip into a bowl and add the rest of the caster sugar, butter, flour, eggs (lightly beat these first) and baking powder. Beat this mixture with a whisk until smooth and creamy.

7. Divide the mixture between the two tins and level the surfaces. Bake for 25 minutes or until just firm to touch, then cool on a wire rack.

Assembly

Strain the rhubarb through a sieve to collect the juices. Whip the cream until it begins to stiffen. Drizzle the juices over the sponges and place one on a serving dish. Spread with cream and cover with rhubarb pieces. Place the second sponge on top and lightly dust with icing sugar.

Tiramisù by Princi

Preparation time

4 hours

Ingredients

For the savoiardi (sponge fingers):

160g egg whites

250g sugar

160g egg yolks

280g flour

Zest of 1 lemon

1 vanilla pod, seeds scraped out

Icing sugar

For the cream:

120g egg yolks

120g sugar

400g mascarpone

1 vanilla pod, seeds scraped out

10g gelatine, melted in a little rum

A little rum

400g cream, whipped

To finish:

Good-quality cocoa powder

600g warm espresso

Method

1. Preheat the oven to 180°C (350°F).

2. To make the savoiardi, whisk 160g of egg whites while slowly adding 250g of sugar.

3. Add 160g of egg yolks, then fold in the flour, lemon zest and vanilla seeds.

4. Pour the mix into a piping bag and pipe fingers 10-12cm long onto a baking tray.

5. Sprinkle the fingers with icing sugar and bake for about 15 minutes.

6. To make the cream, whip 120g egg yolks and 120g sugar together until smooth.

7. Fold in the mascarpone and vanilla seeds.

8. Add the gelatine melted in a little bit of rum and fold in the whipped cream.

Assembly

1. Soak the savoiardi in warm espresso. In a dessert dish, make a layer of savoiardi and top with cream. Repeat this process for one more layer.

2. Refrigerate for at least 3 hours, then sprinkle with cocoa powder to finish.

Vanilla Macaroon by Yauatcha

Cooking time

40 minutes

Ingredients

250g ground almonds

250g icing sugar

180g fresh egg whites kept at room
temperature for 24 hours

250g sugar

75ml water

1g egg white powder

1 vanilla pod, scraped

Method

1. Preheat the oven to 180°C (350°F).

2. Sieve the ground almonds and icing sugar,
then mix well.

3. Add 90g of fresh egg whites to make a
temps per temps.

4. Make an Italian meringue with the remaining
90g egg whites, egg white powder and vanilla
seeds.

5. Fold the meringue through the temps per
temps and beat until slightly slackened.

6. Pipe onto paper-lined trays and leave to skin
for about 30 minutes.

7. Bake for about 7 minutes, then turn the tray
and bake for an additional 3 minutes, or until
the macaroon comes easily off the paper.

Glossary

Afternoon Tea: Light mid-afternoon meal of tea and sandwiches or cakes.

Almond Paste: Paste made from a mixture of finely ground almonds and sugar.

Angel Food Cake: Lightly coloured and textured sponge cake made of egg whites, sugar and flour.

Bakewell Tart: Traditional pastry or shortcrust with a jam and almond sponge filling.

Baking Chocolate: Unsweetened chocolate used for baking.

Basket Weave: Piping pattern made of interwoven horizontal and vertical lines.

Battenberg: Rectangular-shaped sponge cake made up of four square sections, two coloured pink and two coloured yellow, with an outer coating of marzipan.

Batter: Mixture containing flour or starch, used to make breads and cakes.

Bavarian Cream: Light and cold dessert of gelatin with whipped cream and custard sauce or fruit.

Black Forest Gateau: Chocolate and liquor cake with layers of whipped cream and maraschino cherries.

Black-Bottom Cake: Cheescake-like baked dessert with a chocolate base and cream cheese layer.

Blackout: Dark chocolate layer cake, iced with dark chocolate pudding and chocolate crumbs.

Blondie: Light coloured brownie containing vanilla or butterscotch.

Bundt Cake: Ring-shaped cake made in a fluted tube pan called a Bundt pan.

Butter Cakes: Baked cake in which butter is the main ingredient. Other ingredients include sugar, eggs and flour.

Buttercream: A soft mixture, typically of butter and powdered sugar, used as a filling or topping for a cake

Butterfly Cake: see Cupcake.

Canelé: French pastry with a hard caramelised cylindric shell and soft custard centre.

Caramel: Sugar or syrup heated until it turns brown.

Castella: Sponge made of sugar, flour, eggs and starch syrup.

Chantilly Cream: Whipped cream flavoured with vanilla.

Charlotte: Dessert made from lining a mould with bread, sponge cake or biscuits and filled with cream, custard, fruit or sometimes mousse. A Charlotte Royale is made with multi-layers of sponge and jam and a Charlotte Russe with ladyfingers as the surrounding.

Cheesecake: Dessert consisting of a layer of sweetened soft cheese mixed with cream and eggs on a biscuit-crumb or pastry base.

Chiffon Method: A cake mixing method involving the folding of whipped egg whites into a batter made of flour, egg yolks and oil.

Choux: see Pâte à Choux.

Cobbler: Traditional dish taking the form of a pie with no bottom crust.

Coffee Cake: Type of cake traditionally eaten alongside coffee. A coffee cake need not contain coffee.

Compote: Fruit cooked in a sugar syrup, often served as an accompaniment to cakes and brownies.

Cornelli Lace: Piping tecnhnique which produces a lace-like pattern.

Cream of Tartar: Salt potassium bitartrate, used to hold beaten egg whites and to harden flowed sugar.

Cream Tea: Traditional snack from Devon and Cornwall of tea served with scones, jam and cream.

Crème Anglaise: French version of custard, usually flavoured with vanilla.

Crème Chiboust: see St. Honoré Cream.

Crème Pattissiere: see Pastry Cream.

Crème Plombières: Crème Chiboust or Crème Saint-Honoré which has been mixed with fruit.

Croquembouche: Tall cone formed of rings of choux filled with pastry cream and decorated with caramel, almonds, ribbons, flowers or chocolate. A popular alternative to a white wedding cake.

Cupcakes: Cake sized for one, baked in a thin paper cup, named both for the method of using cup-measurements and for the containers originally baked in.

Devil's Food Cake: Rich, moist chocolate layer cake containing ingredients including cocoa, hot water and baking soda thought to be the opposite of the angel food cake.

Dragees: Edible sugar balls coated silver or gold.

Fairy Cake: Small light cake, often with icing and two wing-shaped sponges on top.

Figure Piping: Technique to form figures from icing.

Filo Pastry: A type of pastry made into thin, almost transparent layers.

Flat Icing: Simple icing made using ingredients including powdered sugar, water and sometimes flavourings.

Foam Cake: Cake based on flour, sugar and eggs (instead of butter) which use trapped air through beating, folding and sieving in their preparation to give them their shape, instead of being leavened by yeast.

Foam Icing: Essentially a sweet meringue, it is light, soft and fluffy.

Fondant Icing: Elegant icing with a porcelain look, made from ingredients including sugar, water, glucose or cream of tartar to produce crystallisation.

Frangipane: Almond flavoured cream.

French Fancy: English take on France's Petits-Fours, it is a cube of sponge cake with a hemisphere of buttercream on top, all coated in fondant icing and often drizzled with another colour.

Frosting: A sweet food used to cover or fill cakes, made from sugar and water or sugar and butter. Arguably the distinction between icing and frosting is that frosting is fluffier, thicker and creamier; while icing is thinner, more rigid and glossier.

Fruit Cake: Cake containing candied fruit, dried nuts, fruits and spices; often soaked in spirits and traditionally decorated with white icing at Christmas.

Fudge Icing: Thick and rich icing with a strong chocolate flavour.

Ganache: Rich mix of chocolate and heavy cream, denser than mousse but not as thick as fudge.

Gateau: The French word for cake, but also commonly used to refer to fancier, richer sponge cakes, typically layered with cream or fruit and icing.

Genoise: Classic European sponge cake named after the Italian city of Genoa. It is drier and less sweet than other sponges, and is often soaked in flavoured syrup.

Glaze Icing: Thin, watery icing brushed or poured over pastry to form a crisp shell. A glaze adds flavour and keeps the pastry moist.

High Tea: Substantial meal in the early evening consisting of traditional British dishes such as steak and kidney pie, Cornish pasties and Welsh rarebit. As well as other meat and fish dishes, it often included crumpets, buns, biscuits and pastries alongside a pot of tea.

Japonaise: Baked meringue flavoured with nuts.

Kernel Paste: Paste of apricot kernels and sugar.

Ladyfinger: Named for its shape, a dry sponge cake which can also be considered a biscuit.

Lamington: Popular sponge cake in Australasia, although its origins are unclear. It is known for its coating of chocolate icing and coconut.

Layer Cake: Cake made in layers bound

together by a filling such as cream or jam.

Levelling: Removing the uneven top of a cake before icing and decorating.

Low Tea: See Afternoon Tea.

Macaron: Sweet confectionary consisting of two "cookies" sandwiched around buttercream or jam. The cookies are made primarily from egg whites, sugar and almond paste, and are often coloured or flavoured. Also spelt Macaroon.

Macaroon: Small cookie composed chiefly of egg whites, sugar, and ground almonds or coconut.

Madeira: Traditional English sponge cake with a firm yet light texture, often served with tea and flavoured with lemon.

Madeleine: Traditional French Genoise sponge cake, shaped liked shells and flavoured with nuts or lemon zest.

Marble: Using two colours of cake batter (or icing) to form decorative swirls.

Mille-Feuilles: French dessert of three layers of puff pastry alternated with pastry cream, whipped cream or jam. They are usually topped with glazed icing, fondant with white and chocolate stripes, icing sugar or cocoa.

Mousse: Light and airy filling with a similar texture to dense whipped cream, usually flavoured with chocolate or fruit.

Napoleon: Layers of puff pastry filled with pastry cream.

Nonpareil: Decorative candies for cakes and cookies or a chocolate sweet coated in sugar beads.

Nougat: Mix of ground hazelnuts, sugar and chocolate often used in confectionary.

Pastry Cream: Rich cooked custard, often flavoured and used in éclairs and cakes.

Pâte à Choux: Light pastry with a crisp shell, moist lining and hollow centre, used in profiteroles and éclairs.

Pâte Brisée: Shortcrust pastry used in tarts and pie crusts which does not rise when baked.

Pâte Sablée: Rich and crumbly shortcrust pastry, sweeter than even pâte sucrée.

Pâte Sucrée: Used for baked-in crusts such as cheesecake and tarts, it is more sugary and less fragile than pâte brisée.

Pavlova: Dessert made of meringue, with a crisp crust but a soft, sweet centre. It is usually served with whipped cream and fruit.

Petits-Four: Cake made in layers bound together by a filling such as cream or jam.

Phyllo Pastry: See Filo Pastry.

Piping: When decorative details are produced by pushing icing or cream from a pastry bag through a metal tip.

Pound Cake: Cake traditionally made with a pound of butter, flour, eggs and sugar. The resulting cake is so large that usually the 1:1:1:1 ratio is kept to without actually using a pound of each ingredient.

Puff Pastry: Light, flaky and puffy pastry due to the process of layering in fat while folding the pastry, creating air pockets when the fat melts. It is used in sausage rolls and croissants, although in a modified form. The traditional English method to make it is notoriously difficult, but cheats are often used.

Red Velvet Cake: Traditional American cake, reddish brown in colour due to beet juice and cocoa in the cake mix. It is usually served with thick, white icing and is often made as a layer cake or cupcake.

Royal Icing: Thicker icing which hardens to become brittle.

Sabayon: Very light whipped custard made with sweet wine.

Scone: Also called "rock cakes", a scone is a biscuit-like bread traditionally served with jam and clotted cream for afternoon tea.

Sheet Cake: Cake with one layer, often decorated.

Shortcrust Pastry: The most common and basic form of pastry, it is very versatile as it does not puff up in baking.

Shortening: Solid fat formulated for baking or deep drying, it is white and tasteless.

Sponge Cake: see Foam Cake.

St. Honoré Cream: Pastry cream lightened with whipped cream, and often piped through a St. Honoré tip to create a ridge. Named after the French patron saint of bakers, St. Honoré also gives his name to an elaborate cake.

Sweet Condensed Milk: Made by boiling 60% of the water from a mixture of whole milk and sugar, forming a thick, sweet liquid.

Swiss Roll: Thin sponge cake which is spread with cream and jam, and rolled to create a cylinder.

Tea: Ambiguous term usually used to refer to a small afternoon meal or a light dinner. Traditionally, as high tea was a working class meal and afternoon tea primarily for the upper classes, the word "tea" would be used interchangeably. In modern times such a distinction is no longer true.

Tea Cake: Used to refer to bread or cake that is traditionally served with afternoon tea.

Tea Party: Formal gathering for afternoon tea.

Trifle: Multi-layered dessert with cake, jam, custard, fruit and whipped cream on top.

Upside-Down Cake: Cake which is baked upside-down, in a pan with a rounded bottom and often lined with fruit which forms a decorative top when served.

Victoria Sponge: Common sponge cake named after Queen Victoria. It is characterised by a layer of jam and cream sandwiched between two cakes, but the top of the cake is left plain.

Viennoiserie: When laminated pastry dough is used to form breakfast pastries (such as croissants and brioche). It is a cross between savoury bread baking and pastry making.

Whoopie Pie: American baked treat (arguably more of a cake or cookie than a pie) of buttercream sandwiched between two domes of thick chocolate cake. They are allegedly named after the exclamation that farmers would shout when they saw the treats in their lunchboxes, and are thought to have been initially made out of the leftover batter from making a cake, explaining its heavier texture.

Venues A-Z